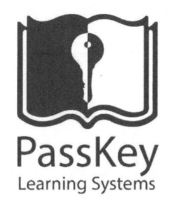

## PassKey
Learning Systems

# *EA Review: Part 1*
# *Single Course Workbook*

## Three Complete
## IRS Enrolled Agent Practice Exams
# Individuals

*May 1, 2024 - February 28, 2025*

*Testing Cycle*

Joel Busch, CPA, JD

Christy Pinheiro, EA, ABA®

Thomas A. Gorczynski, EA, USTCP

**Executive Editor: Joel Busch, CPA, JD**

**Contributors:**

Joel Busch, CPA, JD

Christy Pinheiro, EA, ABA®

Thomas A. Gorczynski, EA, USTCP

*PassKey Learning Systems EA Review Part 1 Workbook: Three Complete IRS Enrolled Agent Practice Exams for Individuals (May 1, 2024-February 28, 2025 Testing Cycle)*

**ISBN 13: 978-1-935664-96-3**

First Printing. April 9, 2024.

Official website: ***www.PassKeyOnline.com***

**This workbook is designed for exam candidates who will take their exams in the May 1, 2024, to February 28, 2025, testing cycle.**

**Note:** Prometric will NOT TEST on any legislation or court decisions passed after December 31, 2023. For exams taken between May 1, 2024, to February 28, 2025, all references on the examination are to the Internal Revenue Code, forms and publications, as amended through December 31, 2023. Also, unless otherwise stated, all questions relate to the calendar year 2023. Questions that contain the term 'current tax year' refer to the calendar year 2023.

*This page intentionally left blank.*

# Table of Contents

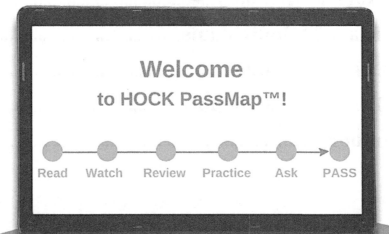

# Recent Praise for the PassKey EA Review Series

*(Real customers, real names, public testimonials)*

**Perfect review book!**

**A. Bergman**

The [PassKey] EA Review is great! Goes into detail and explains why. When you do the practice test, it actually tells you details of the answer for learning and retaining! Definitely recommend!

**Fantastic textbooks and video resources.**

**Vino Joseph Philip**

Comprehensive and accurate video lessons are available online, and testing is also available for each course. I passed all three exams on the first attempt after using Passkey's resources.

**Helped me to pass faster**

**Mohamed Helemish**

I highly recommend Passkey if you are looking for something simple, and easy to understand, and if you want a good reference for your future career in taxes. I passed the exam with confidence and I used it with the three parts.

**I Highly recommend these materials**

**Tosha H. Knelangeon**

Using only the [PassKey] study guide and the workbook, I passed all three EA exams on my first try. I highly recommend these materials. As long as you put in the time to read and study all the information provided, you should be well-prepared.

**I passed on the first try.**

**Jake Bavaro**

I recently passed the first part of the EA exam using just the textbook and a separate practice test workbook. The textbook is very easy to read and understand. Although I have a background in accounting and tax, someone with little or no knowledge of either should be able to grasp all of the various topics covered in the book. I really do believe that it is a superior preparation resource.

**I passed all three parts the first time taking them.**

**Sheryl Reinecke**

I passed all three parts the first time. I read each chapter and the review quiz at the end of each chapter. Before taking the real exam, I did the practice exams in the additional workbook. I feel the material adequately prepared me for success in passing the exam.

**You can pass.**
**Vishnu Kali Osirion**
I really rushed studying for this section. These authors make tax law relevant to your day-to-day experiences and understandable. You can pass the exam with just this as a resource. I do recommend purchasing the workbook as well, just for question exposure. The questions in the book and in the workbook are pretty indicative of what's on the exam. This is a must-buy. Cheers.

**Absolute Best Purchase**
**Sharlene D.**
This book was definitely worth the purchase. The layout was great, especially the examples! Reading the book from front to back allowed me to pass [Part 2]. I also recommend purchasing the workbook or subscribing to the material on their website for this section.

**Excellent explanations!**
**Janet Briggs**
The best thing about these books is that each answer has a comprehensive explanation about why the answer is correct. I passed all three EA exams on the first attempt.

**PassKey was the only study aid that I used**
**Stephen J Woodard, CFP, CLU, ChFC**
The [PassKey] guides were an invaluable resource. They were concise and covered the subject matter succinctly with spot-on end-of-chapter questions that were very similar to what I encountered on the exams.

**Amazing!**
**Sopio Svanishvilion**
PassKey helped me pass all three parts of the Enrolled Agent exam. They are a "must-have" if you want to pass your EA exams.

**I passed all three with Passkey.**
**Swathi B.R.**
I went through the online membership, read the whole book, solved all the questions, and passed the EA exam on my first attempt. For all three [parts], I referred to Passkey EA Review. Wonderful books.

**Passed all 3 Parts!**
**Kowani Collins**
Thank you so much for providing this resource! I have passed all 3 parts of the SEE exam. PassKey allowed me to study on my own time and take the exam with confidence. Thank you for providing such thorough and easy-to-follow resources!

# Introduction

This PassKey EA Review Individuals Workbook is designed to accompany the PassKey EA Review study guide for Individuals, which presents a comprehensive overview of the material you must learn to pass Part 1 of the IRS Special Enrollment Exam (SEE), commonly called the EA exam. This workbook features three complete enrolled agent practice exams, specifically created for the EA exam cycle that runs from **May 1, 2024, to February 28, 2025**.

Each sample exam has 100 questions, similar to the ones you will encounter when you take your actual exam. These test questions are all unique and not found in the PassKey study guides. This is intentional so EA candidates can have a more true-to-life test-taking experience when they go through the workbook questions.

Any EA exam candidate will benefit from the exam questions and detailed answers in this workbook. We suggest that you use it as a study tool to prepare for the exam in a realistic setting. Set aside an uninterrupted block of time and test yourself, just as you would if you were actually taking the EA exam at a testing center.

Score yourself at the end, and then review the answers carefully. Unlike the Prometric exam, you will have a complete, clear answer for each question. If you miss a question, you will know why. Use this workbook to uncover your weak points and improve in those areas. You should answer at least 80% of the questions correctly. Any score below 80% means you need to study more.

All of the questions in the workbook are based on **2023 tax law**, which corresponds with the current EA exam cycle. If you have any questions about the actual exam or if you want to sign up for it, go directly to the Prometric website at *www.prometric.com/IRS*. If you would like to find out more about the PassKey EA Review study program and other learning products by PassKey Publications, visit our website at *www.passkeypublications.com*.

Successfully passing the EA exam can launch you into a fulfilling and lucrative new career. The exam requires intense preparation and diligence, but with the help of PassKey's EA Review, you will have the tools you need to learn how to become an enrolled agent.

As the authors of the PassKey EA Review, we wish you much success!

*This page intentionally left blank.*

# Essential Tax Law Figures for Individuals

Here is a quick summary of some important tax figures for the enrolled agent exam cycle that runs from May 1, 2024, to February 28, 2025.

**Study Note: The IRS has stated in the most recent version of the official Prometric SEE Candidate Bulletin that candidates should not take into account any legislation or court decisions made after December 31, 2023.**

**Legislation Affecting the 2023 Tax Year:**

- The ***SECURE Act 2.0*** was signed into law on December 29, 2022, as part of the *Consolidated Appropriations Act of 2023.* The Act included dozens of provisions affecting retirement plans. Most of the provisions in the SECURE Act 2.0 went into effect in 2023.

- The ***Corporate Transparency Act (the "CTA")*** was enacted by Congress as part of the National Defense Authorization Act. The CTA establishes a beneficial ownership reporting requirement for corporations, limited liability companies, and other similar entities formed or registered to do business in the United States. Starting on January 1, 2024, the CTA will mandate certain types of entities to submit a beneficial ownership information (BOI) report to the Financial Crimes Enforcement Network (FinCEN). Note that according to the testing specifications for the EA exam for this testing window, BOI reports are not included as a testable item on the exam.

**Individual Income Tax Return Filing Deadline: April 15, 2024.**[1] Taxpayers residing in Maine or Massachusetts have until **April 17, 2024,** because of the Patriots' Day and Emancipation Day holidays in those states. The extended filing deadline is **October 15, 2024.**

**FBAR Due Date:** The due date for the FBAR (FinCen 114, Report of Foreign Bank and Financial Accounts) coincides with the filing of the federal tax return. An automatic 6-month extension is allowed, typically until October 15.[2] FBARs must be timely e-filed separately from federal tax returns, on the FinCEN website.

**2023 Tax Rates and Brackets:** The individual tax rates for 2023 for U.S. citizens and U.S. residents are: 10%, 12%, 22%, 24%, 32%, 35%, and 37%. Nonresident aliens filing Form 1040-NR are taxed at a flat 30% rate on US-sourced income unless a tax treaty specifies a lower rate.

---

[1] Taxpayers are automatically granted a 2-month extension of time to file (to June 15) if the taxpayer lives outside the U.S. and their tax home is outside the U.S.

[2] FBAR refers to FinCEN Form 114, Report of Foreign Bank and Financial Accounts, that must be filed with the Financial Crimes Enforcement Network (FinCEN), which is a bureau of the Treasury Department. The FBAR is not filed with the IRS, but the IRS is responsible for FBAR enforcement.

**2023 Standard Deduction Amounts (by Filing Status):**

- Single/MFS: $13,850
- MFJ or QSS: $27,700
- Head of Household: $20,800
- Additional Standard Deduction for Age 65 and over and/or blindness
  - MFJ, QSS or MFS: $1,500
  - Single or HOH: $1,850

**2023 Filing Thresholds Based on Filing Status and Gross Income**

| Filing Status | Age | Filing Threshold |
|---|---|---|
| Single | Under 65 | $13,850 |
| | 65 or older | $15,700 |
| Married Filing Joint and Qualifying Surviving Spouse (QSS) | Under 65 (both spouses) | $27,700 |
| | 65 or older (one spouse) | $29,200 |
| | 65 or older (both spouses) | $30,700 |
| Married Filing Separate | Any age | $5 (not a typo) |
| Head of Household | Under 65 | $20,800 |
| | 65 or older | $22,650 |
| Any filing status | The taxpayer had net earnings from self-employment of at least $400.[3] | |
| Any filing status | Church employee income of $108.28 or more. | |

**2023 Retirement Plan Contribution Limits:** Roth and traditional IRAs: $6,500 (additional catch-up contribution of $1,000 for taxpayers age 50 or older).[4]

**Qualified Small Employer HRA Limits (QSEHRA):** $5,850 Single/ $11,800 family coverage.

**2023 "Kiddie Tax" Threshold:** The "Kiddie Tax" age limit is for those under 18 and certain dependents under 24. The unearned income threshold is $2,500. The kiddie tax only applies to unearned income.[5]

---

[3] Table source: Publication 501, Filing Requirements for Most Taxpayers. Taxpayers who have gross income under these thresholds may still be required to file a return. This chart is not comprehensive. There are situations where a taxpayer may be required to file a return, even with income below these thresholds, for example, if the taxpayer owes special taxes, or those who received advanced payments of the premium tax credit (APTC).

[4] ROTH IRAs: Starting in 2023, SIMPLE and SEP IRAs may now accept Roth contributions. Previously, SIMPLE IRAs and SEP IRAs could only accept pre-tax funds.

[5] The kiddie tax is reported on Form 8615, which is attached to the child's Form 1040. Alternatively, parents can elect to include the child's unearned income directly on their own return, using Form 8814, if certain requirements are met.

**2023 Maximum Compensation Subject to FICA**

- OASDI maximum wage base: $160,200[6]

- Employee and employer portion: 7.65% (6.2% Social Security + 1.45% Medicare)

- Self-employed 15.30% (12.4% Social Security + 2.9% Medicare)

- Additional Medicare Tax: 0.9% on earned income exceeding the following thresholds:

  - Married filing jointly: $250,000[7]
  - Married filing separately: $125,000
  - Single, HOH, and QSS: $200,000

**2023 Capital Gains and Long-Term Dividends:** Short-term capital gains and ordinary dividends are taxed at ordinary income rates. The top rates for qualified dividends and long-term capital gains are as follows:

| Long-Term Capital Gains & Qualified Dividends Tax Rates for 2023 | | | |
|---|---|---|---|
| **Filing status** | **0% rate** | **15% rate** | **20% rate** |
| Single | Up to $44,625 | $44,626 – $492,300 | $492,301 and over |
| Married filing joint & QSS | Up to $89,250 | $89,251 – $553,850 | $553,851 and over |
| Married filing separately | Up to $44,625 | $44,626 – $276,900 | $276,901 and over |
| Head of household | Up to $59,750 | $59,751 – $523,050 | $523,051 and over |
| Trust & Estates | Up to $3,000 | $3,001 - $14,650 | $14,651 and over |
| **Other long-term gains rates** | | | |
| Gain on sale of collectibles | Maximum 28% | | |
| Unrecaptured Sec. 1250 gain | Maximum 25% | | |

**2023 Net Investment Income Tax:** A 3.8% tax applies to individuals, estates, and trusts with net investment income above certain threshold amounts. The MAGI thresholds are:

- Married filing jointly and Qualifying Surviving Spouse: $250,000
- Single and HOH: $200,000
- Married filing separately: $125,000
- Estates and trusts: $14,450

---

[6] "OASDI" is the official name for Social Security in the United States, and the terms are often used interchangeably. The acronym stands for "Old-Age, Survivors, and Disability Insurance." Church employee income is wages received as an employee of a church or qualified church-controlled organization that has a certificate in effect electing an exemption from employer social security and Medicare taxes.

[7] Earned income of spouses is combined towards this Additional Medicare Tax threshold for MFJ returns. Employers must withhold this tax from wages or compensation when they pay employees more than $200,000 in a calendar year, regardless of the employee's filing status.

**2023 Foreign Earned Income Exclusion:** $120,000 per person.

**2023 Bonus Depreciation and Section 179:** Bonus Depreciation ramps down to 80% starting January 1, 2023. In 2023, the maximum Section 179 expense deduction is **$1,160,000.** This limit is reduced by the amount by which the cost of Section 179 property placed in service during the tax year exceeds **$2,890,000.** Once qualifying Section 179 assets placed in service during the year exceed **$4,050,000,** the Section 179 election is no longer available.[8]

**2023 QBI deduction Limits:** The Section 199A limitation phase-in ranges increased and are as follows:

- Married Filing Joint: $364,200-$464,200
- All other filing statuses: $182,100-$232,100

**2023 Standard Mileage Rates:**

- Business use: 65.5 cents a mile
- Medical and moving: 22 cents a mile
- Charitable: 14 cents a mile

**2023 HSA Limits:** To qualify to contribute to a health savings account, the taxpayer must have a high-deductible health insurance policy. The plan must also have an annual limit on out-of-pocket expenses (not including premiums).[9]

| HSA contribution limit (employer + employee) | Self-only: $3,850<br>Family: $7,750 |
|---|---|
| HDHP minimum deductibles | Self-only: $1,500<br>Family: $3,000 |
| HDHP maximum out-of-pocket amounts (not including insurance premiums) | Self-only: $7,500<br>Family: $15,000 |

**2023 FSA Limits:**

- Health Care FSA (HCFSA): $3,050
- Dependent Care FSA (DCFSA): $5,000 for unmarried filers and couples filing jointly, and $2,500 for MFS filers.

**2023 QSEHRA Limits:** Maximum payments and reimbursements through the QSEHRA are: $5,850 for an employee only and $11,800 for an employee plus family.

---

[8] Section 179 and bonus depreciation are covered more extensively in the PassKey EA Review Part 2, Businesses.
[9] The IRS also announced an increase to the Excepted Benefit HRA (EBHRA), which is now $1,950. An EBHRA stands for Excepted Benefit HRA. It is a health reimbursement arrangement that pays qualified medical expenses for excepted benefits like dental and vision coverage. This can be offered in addition to group health coverage. An employee can participate in an EBHRA, even if they decline participation in the employer's group health plan.

**2023 Long-Term Care Premiums Maximum Deduction (Per Person):** The maximum amount of qualified long-term care premiums includible as medical expenses has increased. The limit on the deduction for premiums is for *each* person (not per tax return). Long-term care premiums up to the amounts below can be included as medical expenses on Schedule A.

| Taxpayer's Age At the End of Tax Year | Deductible Limit |
|---|---|
| 40 or less | $480 |
| More than 40 but not more than 50 | $890 |
| More than 50 but not more than 60 | $1,790 |
| More than 60 but not more than 70 | $4,770 |
| More than 70 | $5,960 |

**2023 Alternative Minimum Tax (AMT) Exemption Amounts:**
- Single or Head of Household: $81,300
- Married filing jointly or QSS: $126,500
- Married filing separately: $63,250
- Estates and Trusts: $28,400

**2023 AMT Exemption Beginning Phaseout Range:**
- Single or Head of Household: $578,150 to $ 903,350
- Married filing jointly or QSS: $1,156,300 to $ 1,662,300
- Married filing separately: $578,150 to $831,150
- Estates and Trusts: $94,600 to $208,200

**2023 Estate and Trust *Exemption* Amounts**
- Estates: $600[10]
- Simple trusts: $300
- Complex trusts: $100
- Qualified disability trusts: $4,700

**2023 Estate and Gift Tax Exclusion Amounts**
- Estate and gift tax (highest rate): 40%
- Combined Estate tax and lifetime gift/GST exemption: $12.92 million ($25.84 million per married couple).
- Gift tax annual exclusion: $17,000
- Annual exclusion for gifts to noncitizen spouse: $175,000

---

[10] For estates and trusts, the exemption amount is not allowed in the entity's final tax year (the year of dissolution).

**2023 Retirement Savings Contributions Credit (Saver's Credit):** This credit[11] is between 10% to 50% of eligible contributions to IRAs and qualifying retirement plans up to a maximum credit of $1,000 ($2,000 MFJ). The income limitations are as follows:

| Credit % | MFJ | HOH | All other filers |
|---|---|---|---|
| 50% | AGI not more than $43,500 | AGI not more than $32,625 | AGI not more than $21,750 |
| 20% | $43,501- $47,500 | $32,626 - $35,625 | $21,751 - $23,750 |
| 10% | $47,501 - $73,000 | $35,626 - $54,750 | $23,751 - $36,500 |
| No Credit | more than $73,000 | more than $54,750 | more than $36,500 |

---

[11] The IRS uses two different names for this particular credit: the "Saver's Credit" and the "Retirement Savings Contribution Credit." However, they are the same credit.

# 2023 Tax Credit Changes

**2023 Earned Income Tax Credit (EITC)**

- **Investment income:** The investment income limit in 2023 is $11,000. The investment income limitation is now increased and indexed for inflation.
- **Social Security Numbers:** Taxpayers with valid Social Security numbers can claim the credit, even if their children do not have SSNs. In this instance, they would get the smaller credit available to taxpayers without qualifying children (the "childless EITC"). In the past, these filers did not qualify for the credit.
- **Special rule for separated spouses.** Taxpayers who file married filing separately may qualify for the EITC in limited circumstances (explained later).

| Children Claimed | Maximum AGI (all filing statuses except MFJ) | Maximum AGI (MFJ filers only) |
|---|---|---|
| Zero ("childless EITC") | $17,640 | $24,210 |
| One | $46,560 | $53,120 |
| Two | $52,918 | $59,478 |
| Three or more | $56,838 | $63,398 |

**Maximum amount of the EITC in 2023:**
- No qualifying children: $600 (the "childless EITC")
- 1 qualifying child: $3,995
- 2 qualifying children: $6,604
- 3 or more qualifying children: $7,430[12]

**2023 Child and Dependent Care Credit (CDCTC):** The Child and Dependent Care Credit or "Daycare credit" is a percentage ranging between 20% to 35% of up to $3,000 in qualifying expenses (for one dependent) or $6,000 (for two or more dependents). This credit is not refundable in 2023.

**2023 Child Tax Credit (CTC):** The maximum Child Tax Credit in 2023 is $2,000 per qualifying child. The Additional Child Tax Credit is the refundable component, of which a maximum of $1,600 is refundable in 2023. The CTC phaseout begins at $400,000 (MFJ) and $200,000 for all other filing statuses.

---

[12] The IRS cannot issue refunds claiming the Earned Income Tax Credit (EITC) and the Additional Child Tax Credit (ACTC) before mid-February. This is a congressional provision in the Protecting Americans from Tax Hikes (PATH) Act. This time frame applies to the entire refund, not just the portion associated with these credits.

**2023 Adoption Credit:** $15,950. The AGI phaseout range starts at $239,230 and ends at $279,230 for all filing statuses.[13] The exclusion for employer-paid adoption reimbursement is the same. The adoption credit applies per each adopted child. It is non-refundable, but any unused credit can be carried forward for five years.

**2023 Credit for Other Dependents/Other Dependent Credit (ODC):** The ODC is a tax credit available to taxpayers for dependents who do not qualify for the Child Tax Credit. The maximum credit amount is $500 for each dependent. There is no refundable portion.

**2023 Premium Tax Credit:** The American Rescue Plan Act temporarily removed the 400% FPL ceiling (commonly called the "subsidy cliff") and increased the amount of the credit to qualifying households. For 2023, the repayment caps range from $350 to $3,000, depending on the taxpayer's income and filing status. The ACA subsidy cliff is scheduled to come back in 2026.

**Energy Efficient Tax Credits:** Starting in 2023, the *Inflation Reduction Act* expands two tax credits focused on energy efficiency. Previously called the Nonbusiness Energy Property Credit, the updated credit is now called the *Energy Efficient Home Improvement Credit*. This updated credit can provide a maximum annual credit of $1,200 for qualifying property placed in service during the year. Unlike the previous credit with a lifetime limit of $500, this new one has an increased *annual* limit. Additionally, investments in heat pumps, biomass stoves, and boilers can earn a $2,000 credit.

**New 2023 Clean Vehicle Credit:** The credit for new qualified plug-in electric drive motor vehicles has changed. In 2023, this credit is now known as the *Clean Vehicle Credit*. The maximum amount of the credit and some of the requirements to claim the credit have changed. The credit is reported on Form 8936 and Schedule 3, line 6f.

---

[13] Unlike most other credits, the adoption credit has the same phaseout range for all filing statuses.

# 2023 Education-Related Credits and Deductions

**American Opportunity Credit:** The credit is up to $2,500 per student for the first four years of higher education expenses paid. The credit phases out for unmarried taxpayers with MAGIs between $80,000 and $90,000 ($160,000 and $180,000 for MFJ).

**Lifetime Learning Credit:** 20% of tuition paid up to a credit of $2,000 per return. In 2023, the credit phases out for unmarried taxpayers with MAGIs between $80,000 and $90,000 ($160,000 and $180,000 for MFJ).

**Coverdell Education Savings Accounts (also called an "Education IRA"):** The maximum contribution limit is $2,000 per beneficiary in 2023. Contributions must be made in cash, and are not deductible.

**Section 529 Plans (Qualified Tuition Programs or QTP):** The IRS does not specify a specific dollar amount for annual contribution limits to 529 college savings plans, but contributions are considered gifts for tax purposes and are subject to gift tax limits. This means that in 2023, up to $17,000 per beneficiary qualifies for the annual gift tax exclusion.

**Student loan interest deduction:** Student loan interest includes both required and voluntary interest payments. The maximum deduction per return is $2,500, regardless of filing status. The 2023 phaseout limits are:
- Married filing jointly: $155,000 - $185,000
- Single, HOH, QSS: $75,000 - $90,000
- MFS filers cannot take this deduction.

**Educational Savings Bond Expense Exclusion:** The savings bond education tax exclusion allows taxpayers to exclude interest income upon redeeming eligible savings bonds when the bond owner pays qualified higher education expenses at an eligible institution. This exclusion is subject to the following income limitations in 2023:
- Married filing jointly: $137,800 – $167,800
- Unmarried filers: $91,850 – $106,850
- MFS filers cannot take the deduction.

**Educator Expense deduction:** The deduction for educator expenses, also known as the "teacher credit," is set at $300 for the year 2023. If two teachers are married and file taxes jointly, they can claim a total deduction of $600 ($300 each).

# Other Essential Tax Law Updates for Individuals in 2023

**Insurance premiums for retired public safety officers:** Retired public safety officers can receive a tax break on their retirement distributions. They can exclude up to $3,000 of distributions from income from an eligible retirement plan if the funds are used directly for health insurance premiums.

**Direct File Pilot Program:** Direct File is a new IRS tool that provides taxpayers with relatively simple returns to e-file their federal tax return for free. Taxpayer eligibility to participate in the pilot will be limited to 13 states in the initial pilot, but the IRS plans to expand the service.

**Increase in penalty for failure to file:** The penalty for failure of an individual to file a tax return that is more than 60 days late shall not be less than the lesser of (1) $485 or (2) 100% of the tax due on the return.

**Student Loan Forgiveness:** Exclusion from gross income is available for student loan forgiveness after 2020 and before 2026 for most forgiven student loans. An employer may also contribute up to $5,250 annually toward an employee's student loans. The $5,250 cap applies to both the student loan repayment benefit and other educational assistance (e.g., tuition, fees, books) provided by the employer.

**Required Minimum Distribution Changes:** The SECURE Act 2.0 has changed the rules for RMDs. For 2023, the age at which account owners must start taking required minimum distributions goes up from age 72 to age 73.

**Excess Business Losses:** The *Inflation Reduction Act* extended the provision for excess business losses through 2028. Non-corporate taxpayers, including sole proprietors, are limited in their offset use of overall business losses to offset nonbusiness income. The excess business loss limitation is $578,000 for MFJ, and $289,000 for all other filing statuses in 2023.

**Personal and Dependency Exemptions:** The deduction for all personal exemptions is suspended (reduced to zero) through 2025. For 2023, the gross income limitation[14] for a qualifying relative is $4,700 (also called the "deemed exemption" amount).

**2023 "Nanny Tax" on Household Employees:** The nanny tax threshold is $2,600 in 2023. A household employer is normally obligated to withhold and pay federal FICA (Social Security and Medicare) taxes for any household employee above this threshold. A household employer is required to pay FUTA taxes if they paid a household employee $1,000 or more in a calendar quarter in the current or prior year. These thresholds are on a per-employee basis.

---

[14] A "deemed personal exemption" is used for purposes of determining who is a "qualifying relative" under IRC Sec. 152(d)(1)(B). An exemption amount still applies to Qualified Disability Trusts.

## 2023 Tax Form Changes

**Publication 535, Business Expenses,** is now historical. The 2022 edition will be the final revision available.

**The new Form 7206,** *Self-Employed Health Insurance Deduction,* will be used by self-employed individuals to calculate and claim the deduction for health insurance as an above-the-line deduction.

**Form 1040-X, Amended U.S. Individual Tax Return,** now includes the option to select direct deposit of their refund.

**IRIS Platform for Information Return filings:** The Taxpayer First Act required the IRS to develop an Internet portal that allows taxpayers to file Forms 1099 electronically. On January 25, 2023, this new platform, called the *Information Returns Intake System (IRIS)* went live. Filers must register with the IRS before using IRIS.

**E-file Mandate for Information Returns:** On February 21, 2023, the IRS issued final regulations requiring most businesses to e-file beginning in 2024. This mandate applies to individuals and businesses who submit 10 or more information returns, such as Form 1099, W-2, and 1099-MISC. Failure to e-file, when required, may result in penalties imposed on taxpayers and businesses who file their information returns on paper instead.

**2023 Rules for Form 1099-K:** The reporting requirement for Form 1099-K, Payment Card and Third-Party Network Transactions, was reduced by the *American Rescue Plan of 2021*. However, on November 21, 2023, the IRS announced an additional delay in the new 1099-K reporting threshold for third-party settlement organizations (TPSOs). As a result, reporting will not be required unless the taxpayer receives over $20,000 and has more than 200 transactions in 2023. These reporting requirements do not apply to personal transactions such as birthday or holiday gifts, sharing the cost of a car ride or meal, or paying a family member or another for a household bill.

*This page intentionally left blank.*

# #1 Sample Exam: Individuals

**(Please test yourself first, then check the correct answers at the end of this exam.)**

1. William has a Health Savings Account (HSA) through his employer. In 2023, William contributed $2,300 of his own funds to his HSA. His employer contributes an additional $1,200 to William's HSA, but the employer does not include this amount in his wages. Which of the following statements is true?

A. William may deduct his own contributions as well as his employer's contributions to the HSA as an adjustment to income on his individual return.
B. William has overcontributed to his HSA and is now subject to a 6% excise tax on the excess.
C. William may deduct only his own HSA contributions on his return as an adjustment to income.
D. An employer may not contribute to an employee's HSA unless the amounts are included in taxable wages.

2. Akram is 65 and unmarried. He qualifies for Head of Household filing status because he supports his elderly mother, Mahya, who is 85 years old and lives with him. His mother only has Supplemental Security income (SSI) and does not file a return. Akram had $21,000 in wage income during the year. Is Akram required to file a tax return?

A. Yes, he must file.
B. No, he does not have to file.
C. Depends on his mother's net income.
D. Depends on his state of residence.

3. Clayton works as a notary and independent bookkeeper and has several business clients. His biggest client, Danville Construction Company, sends Clayton a Form 1099-NEC to report he received $22,400 for his bookkeeping services during the year. Clayton also received other cash payments of $2,500 from several different individuals for personal bookkeeping work he completed. He did not receive Forms 1099-NEC for the $2,500. He also received $250 in fees for services he performed as a notary public. Based on this information, how much of his income is subject to regular income tax, and how much is subject to self-employment tax?

A. $22,400 is subject to income tax and self-employment tax. The remaining $2,500 is only subject to regular income tax. Notary fees are not taxable.
B. $22,400 is subject only to income tax. The other $2,500 is subject to income tax and self-employment tax. Notary fees are not taxable.
C. $24,900 is subject to income tax and self-employment tax. The $250 of fees received for services performed as a notary public are subject to income tax, but not self-employment tax.
D. All of his income is subject to self-employment tax and income tax.

4. Jacob works full-time as a grocery store cashier. He is also a competitive cyclist and has regularly participated in cycling competitions for the past six years with the primary intent of having fun, but he can also earn prize winnings. He has devoted significant time and effort to developing expertise in cycling, and he keeps good records that track his income and expenses associated with the competitions. Jacob has not yet earned a profit through the cycling tournaments. As his tax preparer, what would you advise Jacob regarding his cycling activity?

A. The cycling competitions constitute a trade or business activity, so he can deduct his expenses on Schedule C.
B. Jacob is engaging in a hobby, so he can deduct his expenses only up to the amount of his competition income. The expenses are only deductible on Schedule A as a miscellaneous itemized deduction.
C. Jacob cannot deduct any expenses associated with the competitions. However, he must claim any prizes as income.
D. Jacob cannot deduct any expenses but does not have to claim any of the prize income since the activity is not a business.

5. Janelle has the following sources of income during the year. Which of the following types of income must be reported on Schedule 1 as "other income" on her individual tax return?

A. Rental income.
B. Jury duty pay.
C. Social Security retirement income.
D. Wages.

6. Evie receives $40,000 of life insurance coverage as a fringe benefit through her employer. She is also entitled to $100,000 of optional life insurance coverage. This optional benefit is also carried (paid) by her employer and offered to all the employees as part of their cafeteria plan. Evie decides to enroll in the optional life insurance coverage, bringing her coverage amount to $140,000. How much of the insurance cost is excludable as a nontaxable fringe benefit to Evie, and how much would be taxable?

A. The entire cost of the life insurance policy would be excludable from Evie's income as an employee fringe benefit.
B. The cost of the first $40,000 of coverage is excludable, and the remaining amount would be taxable to Evie as wages.
C. The cost of the first $50,000 of coverage is excludable, and the remaining amount would be taxable to Evie as wages.
D. The entire cost of the policy would be taxable as wages to Evie.

7. Vanessa owns stock in several companies and receives distributions from her investments throughout the year. Which of the following corporate distributions will normally be reported on her Form 1040 as taxable income?

A. $100 in capital gain distributions from her mutual fund.
B. A $350 return of capital from Decker Corporation.
C. A 2-for-1 stock split where she receives 150 additional shares.
D. Dividends paid on her cash-value life insurance policy.

8. Corwin withdrew $6,000 from a one-year, deferred-interest certificate of deposit during the year, before the maturity date. As such, he had to pay an early withdrawal penalty of $291. How should this penalty be reported on Corwin's individual tax return?

A. Corwin can deduct the penalty as an adjustment to income on Schedule 1 of Form 1040.
B. Corwin can claim the penalty as a miscellaneous itemized deduction on Schedule A.
C. Corwin can deduct the penalty from his taxable interest on Schedule B.
D. Early withdrawal penalties are never deductible.

9. Walker Smith dies on January 2, 2023. At the time of his death, Walker had several rental properties and other investments that earned income. He dies unmarried and without a will, so his estate must go through probate. In 2023, the Estate of Walker Smith has distributable net income (DNI) of $30,000, consisting of $18,000 of rents and $12,000 of taxable interest. The executor distributes $15,000 each to the two equal beneficiaries, Nadia and Jasmine, who are Walker's adult daughters. How should Nadia and Jasmine report this income on *their* individual tax returns?

A. Each will be treated as having received $15,000 of ordinary income, which would be reported on Schedule C.
B. Each will be treated as having received $9,000 of rental income and $6,000 of taxable interest.
C. Each will be treated as having received $18,000 of rental income and $12,000 of interest.
D. This income does not need to be reported by the beneficiaries because it has already been taxed at the estate level on Form 706.

10. For the purpose of determining filing status, which of the following taxpayers would be considered *unmarried* for the entire tax year?

A. Daisuke, who got married on December 31, 2023.
B. Agnes, whose husband died on November 5, 2023. Agnes did not remarry during the year.
C. Hitoshi, who is married to a nonresident alien.
D. Jason, who was married until his divorce became final on September 14, 2023.

11. Simon is wealthy and financially supports a number of people, all of which live in his household with him all year. Which of the following persons *cannot* be claimed by Simon as his dependent?

A. Tiffany, Simon's niece, age 22, and a full-time student. Tiffany earned $3,500 in wages from a part-time job and has no other income.
B. Waylon, Simon's father, age 76 and has no taxable income.
C. Zayden, age 17, Simon's foster child. Zayden earned $10,200 in wages but did not provide more than one-half of his own support.
D. Allie, who is age 52 and Simon's live-in housekeeper. Simon pays all of Allie's wages and provides her room and board in his home.

12. Which of the following employees would *not* be allowed to deduct their work-related expenses on Form 2106?

A. An Armed Forces reservist.
B. A disabled employee with impairment-related work expenses.
C. An employee of an accounting firm with unreimbursed mileage expenses.
D. A qualified performing artist.

13. Benjamin received 1,000 shares of stock as an inheritance from his grandmother, who died on February 20, 2023. His grandmother's adjusted basis in the stock was $8,000. The stock's fair market value on the date of her death was $24,500. The executor of the estate elects the alternate valuation date for valuing the gross estate. On August 20, 2023, the stock's fair market value was $21,500. Benjamin received the stock on November 26, 2023, when its fair market value was $22,100. Benjamin sells all the stock two weeks later for $22,950. What is Benjamin's basis and holding period in the inherited stock?

A. $8,000 basis, and his holding period is long-term.
B. $21,500 basis, and his holding period is long-term.
C. $22,100 basis, and his holding period is short-term.
D. $24,500 basis, and his holding period is short-term.

14. Kamila is unmarried with no dependents. She dies on November 7, 2023. She was 64 at the time of her death. Her birthday was December 15, so she would have reached 65 years of age if she had lived the entire year. What is Kamila's standard deduction on her final tax return?

A. Her standard deduction would be $13,850 in 2023.
B. Her standard deduction would be $15,700 in 2023.
C. Her standard deduction would be $20,800 in 2023.
D. Her standard deduction would be $0 in 2023, because she is deceased.

15. Gina and Anthony married on August 30, 2023. Earlier in 2023, Anthony had enrolled in an accredited college to earn his first bachelor's degree and subsequently received a Form 1098-T, Tuition Statement. This was the first year Anthony has ever attended college. Gina was employed with wages of $85,000 and paid for all of Anthony's educational expenses. Anthony had no taxable income for the year. Based on their circumstances, can either taxpayer claim the American Opportunity Tax Credit?

A. Anthony is ineligible to claim any education credits because his wife paid his education expenses, and they were not married when the costs were incurred.
B. The spouses must file a joint return to claim the American Opportunity Credit.
C. Based on Gina and Anthony's AGI, they do not qualify to claim an education credit.
D. Gina should deduct the education expenses on Schedule A as a miscellaneous itemized deduction, since they do not qualify to take the expenses as an education credit.

16. Florencia is single and lives in New York. She plans to itemize her deductions this year. She paid the following taxes during the tax year:

- $3,500 in sales tax on a brand-new car.
- $450 in personal property taxes (DMV fees) on the new car.
- $9,000 in property tax on her main home in New York.
- $14,000 in state income tax paid to New York.

What is her maximum deduction on Schedule A for taxes?

A. $5,000
B. $10,000
C. $23,450
D. $26,500

17. Zachary and Annie are married and file jointly. Both are U.S. citizens, and they lived the entire year in the United States. Zachary and Annie have a joint bank account in Jamaica with $198,000 in funds that they deposited on July 10, 2023, when they were trying to purchase a vacation home overseas. The home sale fell through, and the money remained in the account. They did not deposit any additional funds in 2023, and the account did not generate any taxable interest. What is their reporting requirement to the U.S. authorities relating to these funds?

A. None, because they made no new deposits and had no taxable income from the account.
B. They are required to attach a formal disclosure statement to their 1040 tax return.
C. They must file an FBAR and Form 8938.
D. They must file only Form 8938 with the IRS.

18. Jeffrey is a self-employed HVAC repairman who reports his income on Schedule C. His business has two employees, a full-time receptionist and an apprentice who works part-time. Which of the following insurance expenses is not deductible on Jeffrey's Schedule C?

A. Health insurance for Jeffrey, the owner.
B. Health insurance for Jeffrey's two employees.
C. Liability insurance for Jeffrey's business.
D. Auto insurance on Jeffrey's work vehicle.

19. To meet the "substantial presence" test in determining U.S. residency for IRS purposes, an individual without a valid green card must be physically present in the United States for at least _____ days over a three-year period.

A. 120
B. 183
C. 214
D. 365

20. Stetson bought his primary residence on September 1, 2019. He lived in this home until January 30, 2023, when he moved in with his girlfriend. On September 15, 2023, Stetson and his girlfriend decided to get engaged. Consequently, Stetson puts his former house up for sale. On December 27, 2023, Stetson's home sold, and he has an $83,000 gain. Is Stetson required to report any of the profit, and, if so, what is the nature of the gain?

A. He must report $83,000 of long-term capital gain.
B. He must report $83,000 of short-term capital gain.
C. He must prorate the capital gain based on the number of days that he was not living in the home within the last 24 months.
D. All the gain can be excluded from income.

21. Donnie owns a sole proprietorship that refurbishes medical equipment. His machine shop is located in Texas, but Donnie actually lives in Louisiana, right near the Texas border. He also owns several rental properties in Nevada. He pays for a post office box in Nevada to receive and forward his mail. For federal tax purposes, Donnie's "tax home" would probably be determined by:

A. His principal place of business in Texas.
B. His mailing address in Nevada.
C. His physical address in Louisiana.
D. Whatever mailing address is listed on his tax return.

22. Seven years ago, Jerry invested in the stock of a small, domestic C corporation. The stock qualifies as Section 1244 stock. The company did poorly, and Jerry has $50,000 in losses from the sale of his shares. He also earned $129,000 in wages during the year. Which of the following is true?

A. Jerry can deduct $3,000 in long-term capital losses on his individual tax return.
B. Jerry can deduct $3,000 in ordinary losses on his individual tax return.
C. Jerry can deduct $50,000 in ordinary losses on his individual tax return.
D. Jerry can deduct $50,000 in Ponzi losses on his individual tax return.

23. Tatum owns a commercial strip mall that he rents out to business tenants. He reports the income from his rental activity on Schedule E. During the year, Tatum purchased and installed a new fire protection system in the building, which cost $23,400. It was the only asset he placed in service during the year. The strip mall generated $300,000 of rental income. Tatum wants to deduct the entire cost of the fire protection system in 2023, if possible. How should he report this cost on his tax return?

A. Tatum may deduct the entire cost using Section 179.
B. Tatum may deduct the entire cost using straight-line depreciation.
C. Tatum may deduct the entire cost as a normal business expense.
D. Tatum cannot deduct the entire cost in the current year. He must capitalize and depreciate the cost of the fire protection system.

24. Abiram is a nonresident alien taxpayer with U.S.-based investments. He will file a Form 1040-NR to report his U.S. investment income only. Abiram is a citizen of Morocco and donates to many charities in his home country. He also made several donations to Boston University, a qualifying 501(c)(3) organization. Can Abiram deduct his charitable gifts on his Form 1040-NR?

A. No, charitable gifts are not deductible by nonresident aliens.
B. He may deduct his charitable contributions only to U.S. nonprofit organizations.
C. Yes, all of his gifts are deductible, including contributions to charities in his home country.
D. Abiram cannot take a deduction for charitable gifts on his Form 1040-NR, but he may take a tax credit instead.

25. Which form requires U.S. persons to report various types of foreign assets, not just bank accounts?

A. FBAR
B. Form 8938
C. Schedule B
D. Form 8300

26. Kerrie is single with no dependents. On January 1, 2023, Kerrie enrolled through the Marketplace in a qualified health plan for 2023. On July 14, 2023, Kerrie enlisted in the Army and was immediately eligible for government-sponsored coverage, so she canceled her Marketplace coverage at the end of July. For what period is Kerrie able to claim a Premium Tax Credit (assuming she meets all of the eligibility criteria)?

A. The entire tax year.
B. January through June.
C. January through July.
D. She is not eligible for the PTC because she is not enrolled in Marketplace coverage for at least nine months of the tax year.

27. Mai-Lin is single. In 2023, she had $120,000 in wage income. She also owns a residential rental property that has a $28,000 loss for the year. Mai-Lin actively participated in the rental activity but is not considered a real estate professional. How much of her rental loss is deductible in the current year on *Schedule E, Form 1040?*

A. $0
B. $15,000
C. $25,000
D. $28,000

28. Tristan's wife died on July 5, 2022 (the prior year), and he filed a joint tax return for that year with his wife, signing as the surviving spouse. Tristan has not remarried and maintains a home for his two young children, ages 7 and 9, who lived with him all year. He provides all the financial support for his children. What is the best filing status for Tristan in 2023?

A. Single.
B. Head of Household.
C. Married Filing Jointly.
D. Qualifying Surviving Spouse (QSS).

29. Royce sold cryptocurrency in 2023. The sale resulted in a capital loss of $7,000. Royce has wages of $52,000. He has no other income or losses during the year and will file as Single. What is Royce's adjusted gross income?

A. $45,000
B. $49,000
C. $52,000
D. $59,000

30. Dennis is single. He is employed full-time as a video game developer for a large company. He also runs a popular online gaming website, which he operates as a sole-proprietorship. Dennis received the following income in 2023:

| Regular wages | $188,000 |
|---|---|
| Bonus wages from job | $10,000 |
| Net self-employment income from gaming website | $56,000 |
| Interest income on CDs | $3,000 |
| Cash inheritance from his deceased sister | $25,000 |

What amount does he owe for the *Additional Medicare Tax* in 2023 (the threshold is $200,000 for single filers)?

A. $486
B. $558
C. $2,286
D. $9,652

31. Dixie is 29 and single. She is not disabled. On March 11, 2023, she decided to transfer her traditional IRA to another financial institution. She properly initiates the transfer, but the bank makes an error and the transfer is not completed within the required 60-day rollover window. She discovers the bank's mistake and completes the IRA transfer on August 12, 2023. What recourse does Dixie have in this case?

A. Dixie may be eligible for an automatic waiver of the 60-day IRA rollover rule or request a Private Letter Ruling from the IRS.
B. Dixie must pay a 10% early withdrawal penalty. The 60-day IRA rollover window cannot be waived.
C. Dixie must request a Private Letter Ruling from the IRS in order to avoid a penalty.
D. Dixie can avoid the 10% penalty only by appealing the penalty in the U.S. Tax Court.

32. Hayato spends two years working in Germany as a private consultant for a multinational investment company. He is a U.S. green-card holder and a natural citizen of Japan. He was physically present in Germany for 365 days in 2023 (the full year). He has qualified foreign-earned income of $190,000 in 2023. As a green-card holder, he is required to file a U.S. tax return. What is the maximum amount of income he can exclude from U.S. tax using the Foreign Earned Income Exclusion?

A. $13,850
B. $112,000
C. $120,000
D. $190,000

31

33. Tommy is a self-employed building contractor who files a Schedule C. Tommy entertains his best client at a baseball game, and doing so, he secures a lucrative contract. He also takes a different client out to lunch for his birthday. Tommy throws an annual holiday party in December for his ten employees. The holiday party includes a catered buffet and a music DJ. All the employees are invited to the party. In 2023, he had the following meal and entertainment expenses related to his business:

| Expense | Cost |
|---|---|
| Tickets to a baseball game to entertain his client | $196 |
| A business meal at a restaurant with a client | $78 |
| Catering and music for a holiday party for Tommy's 12 employees | $560 |

What is the *allowable* meal deduction expense on his Schedule C?

A. $79
B. $269
C. $417
D. $599

34. Phoebe is 51 years old and has retired on Federal Employees Retirement System (FERS) disability from her postal service job. While loading packages into her mail truck, a large crate fell on her and left her paralyzed. She receives a monthly payment from her former employer's pension plan. Phoebe has not reached the minimum retirement age set by her company's pension plan. How should she report her disability income on her Form 1040?

A. Wages.
B. Social Security income.
C. The amounts are not taxable.
D. Pensions and annuities.

35. Rylie currently owes $79,000 in delinquent Federal student loans. She was not married to her husband, Alfred, when she incurred the debt. Alfred and Rylie file a joint return in 2023, which shows a refund of $5,000. Their entire refund was offset due to Rylie's delinquent student loan debt. Which of the following is a correct statement?

A. Since he filed a joint return with his wife, Alfred has no recourse to claim a portion of the refund. The entire refund will be offset toward Rylie's delinquent student loan debt.
B. Alfred should apply for innocent spouse relief to request his portion of the refund.
C. Alfred should apply for equitable relief to request his portion of the refund be allocated to him.
D. Alfred should apply for injured spouse relief to request his portion of the refund be allocated to him.

36. Katherine is divorced and provided over half the cost of keeping up a home. Her 13-year-old daughter, Danika, lived with her for eight months in 2023. Katherine has signed a written declaration allowing her ex-husband, Troy, to claim Danika as a dependent. Troy will be claiming Danika this year. What filing status should Katherine use?

A. Single.
B. Head of Household.
C. Married Filing Separately.
D. Married Filing Jointly.

37. Under the simplified home office deduction calculation, the maximum deduction amount a taxpayer can claim in 2023 is:

A. $300
B. $500
C. $1,500
D. $3,000

38. Which of the following taxpayers would generally not be considered self-employed and therefore would *not* be subject to self-employment tax?

A. An independent contractor.
B. A general partner of a partnership that operates a trade or business.
C. A taxpayer who owns five residential rentals and reports their rental income on Schedule E.
D. A person who works full-time and also has a part-time business.

39. Which of the following are qualified adoption expenses for purposes of the Adoption Credit?

A. Expenses for adopting a spouse's child.
B. Adoption expenses reimbursed by an employer.
C. A surrogate parenting arrangement.
D. Expenses paid in an unsuccessful attempt to adopt an eligible child.

40. To qualify for the Earned Income Tax Credit, which of the following statements is true?

A. The taxpayer must have a dependent child.
B. The taxpayer must be a U.S. citizen or legal U.S. resident all year with a Social Security Number that is valid for work purposes.
C. If a taxpayer is a full-time student, they cannot qualify for the EITC.
D. The taxpayer must be a U.S. citizen or resident with either a valid Social Security Number or ITIN.

41. Several years ago, Rohan received 10 shares of Valley Telecom, Inc. stock as a gift from his father. His father had originally paid $10 per share for this stock, and it was trading for $20 per share at the time of the gift. On January 15, 2023, Rohan purchased an additional 20 shares of Valley Telecom stock for a price of $30 per share and paid a $20 brokerage fee on this purchase. On October 30, 2023, Rohan sold 20 shares of his Valley Telecom stock. He cannot accurately identify the shares he disposed of. What is Rohan's basis in the shares he still owns?

A. $100
B. $200
C. $310
D. $410

42. Piper, age 26, recently started college for her first undergraduate degree. She receives a $4,750 scholarship from her local church. The scholarship may *only* be used for college tuition. Piper's total tuition cost for the year was $6,800. Piper also paid the following additional educational costs during the year:

| | |
|---|---|
| Required textbooks | $450 |
| Mandatory student health fees | $186 |
| Required lab equipment | $1,260 |
| Commuting costs | $340 |
| Meals on-campus in the cafeteria | $129 |
| Parking tickets at the college | $98 |

Piper wants to claim the American Opportunity Tax Credit (AOTC) on her tax return. Of the items listed above, what are her qualifying educational expenses for purposes of the credit?

A. $2,050
B. $3,760
C. $3,946
D. $8,510

43. Emiko works as a self-employed bookkeeper. During the year, she receives a Form 1099-NEC from one of her bookkeeping clients that shows an incorrect amount. What should she do?

A. Contact the payor for a corrected Form 1099-NEC.
B. Contact IRS for a corrected Form 1099-NEC.
C. Report the amount stated on Form 1099-NEC as income, and then adjust off the incorrect amount as an expense.
D. Disregard Form 1099-NEC since it is incorrect.

44. Staci owns and lives in her main home. She rents a single room in her 1,200 square-foot house to a long-term tenant. The rental room measures 10 feet by 12 feet (120 square feet, or 10% of the total house). What is she allowed to deduct on Schedule E?

A. She may deduct 100% of the expenses that relate only to the rental portion of the house, and 10% of any qualified expenses that apply to the entire house.
B. She may deduct 90% of the expenses that relate only to the rental portion of the house, and 10% of any qualified expenses that apply to the entire house.
C. She may deduct 100% of any qualified expense that apply to the entire house.
D. She may deduct 10% of any qualified expense that relates to her rental activity.

45. Rosalie earned $34,000 in wages in 2023. She also received ordinary dividends in the amount of $175. She also had a $700 capital gain from the sale of stock. How should these items of income be reported?

A. All her investment income should be reported on Form 1040, Schedule B.
B. Rosalie's ordinary dividends should be reported on Form 1040, and the capital gain from the stock sale should be reported on Schedule D.
C. Rosalie's ordinary dividends should be reported on Schedule B, and the capital gain from the stock sale should be reported on Schedule D.
D. Both amounts should be reported on Form 1040, Schedule D.

46. Anwar and Malika are legally married but have lived apart in separate homes since August 10, 2023. They do not have a formal separation agreement and have not filed for divorce. They have one daughter, Leila, who lived with Malika all year. Anwar does not wish to file jointly with Malika. What is the best filing status for Malika if she does not want to have any interactions with Anwar regarding taxes?

A. Single
B. Head of household
C. Married filing separately
D. Married filing jointly

47. Dillon died on July 20, 2023. The value of his assets totaled $19 million when he died, so an estate tax return must be filed (Form 706). Which of the following assets would be included in the calculation of his gross estate on Form 706?

A. Life insurance proceeds payable to Dillon's children.
B. Property owned solely by Dillon's spouse.
C. Lifetime gifts that are complete.
D. All of the items above would be included in Dillon's gross estate.

48. Benita lost her job at the beginning of the year. She missed several mortgage payments on her home and the bank threatened foreclosure. Benita found another job in November, but her salary was less than what she had been earning before. Benita contacted her lender and asked to refinance and obtain a mortgage modification. Rather than go through the expense of a foreclosure, the lender agrees to reduce the principal on Benita's loan and refinance it with a better interest rate and lower payments. The principal balance before November 1, 2023, was $230,000, and the lender reduced the loan to $200,000. The home has never been used for business or as rental property, and Benita has not filed for bankruptcy. Based on this information, how should Benita report this transaction on her tax return?

A. She should report $30,000 as a capital gain on Schedule D.
B. She should report the reduction in the basis of the home on Form 982. The amount is not taxable.
C. She should report the $30,000 as a nondeductible capital loss on Form 8949 and Schedule D.
D. She must include the debt cancellation amount in income.

49. Kelsey owns a residential rental duplex. Both units were vacant at the beginning of the year. On April 1, 2023, Kelsey begins renting the first unit for $1,300 per month. She also collects a $1,000 refundable cleaning deposit from the first tenant. The second unit is being advertised in the local newspaper, but Kelsey is having trouble finding a responsible tenant. On October 1, 2023, Kelsey is finally able to rent the second unit for $600 per month. Kelsey obtains a $300 refundable cleaning deposit from the second tenant. On December 12, 2023, Kelsey's second tenant leaves on vacation and pays his January 2024 rent in advance. Kelsey accepts the check for $600 but does not cash it until January. Based on this information, how much rental income should Kelsey report on her Schedule E for 2023?

A. $13,500
B. $14,100
C. $14,800
D. $15,400

50. Five years ago, Jakob purchased 200 shares of Baxter Steel Corporation stock. On January 10, 2023, Jakob gives his daughter, Becky, the 200 shares of Baxter Steel Corporation stock as a gift. Jakob's adjusted basis in the stock was $950. On the date of the transfer, the fair market value of the stock was $1,100. Becky sells all 200 shares for $1,320 on November 16, 2023. What is the amount and nature of Becky's gain?

A. $150 short-term capital gain.
B. $270 long-term capital gain.
C. $370 short-term capital gain.
D. $370 long-term capital gain.

51. A fire destroyed Chelsea's rental property on January 9, 2023. The property was a total loss. Before the fire, the home had an adjusted basis of $80,000, and the insurance company paid her $130,000 for the loss on November 3, 2023. Chelsea bought a smaller replacement rental home for $100,000 on December 28, 2023. Chelsea used the remaining $30,000 from the insurance reimbursement to pay off her student loans. How much is her taxable gain from this casualty event, and what is her basis in the new rental property?

A. No taxable gain; basis of $130,000.
B. Taxable gain of $30,000; basis of $80,000.
C. Taxable gain of $30,000; basis of $100,000.
D. Taxable gain of $50,000; basis of $100,000.

52. Several years ago, Aileen bought an old painting from a thrift store for $20. She hung it up in her living room. In 2023, Aileen discovers the painting is an expensive original work of art. She takes the painting to an auction house and sells it for $6,000. The auction house takes a 30% commission. What amount must Aileen report as a taxable gain?

A. $4,180
B. $5,000
C. $5,880
D. $6,000

53. Serena has four dependents. She pays all of the household expenses, and none of her dependents have any taxable income. Which of the following dependents would qualify Serena for the Child Tax Credit in 2023?

A. Soren, her 22-year-old son, who is a full-time college student.
B. Elodie, her 19-year-old daughter. She is not a student, but she is permanently disabled.
C. Skye, a 16-year-old foster child attending high school.
D. Susan, 63 years old, Serena's mother and also her dependent parent.

54. On January 1, 2023, Elias bought 1,000 shares of Express Works Inc. stock for $14,800. He also paid an additional $200 in broker's commissions to purchase the stock. On December 31, 2023, he sold 600 shares of the stock for $7,800. What is the amount and nature of his gain or loss?

A. Short-term capital loss of $1,200.
B. Short-term capital gain of $1,300.
C. Long-term capital gain of $1,200.
D. Short-term capital loss of $1,050.

55. Agnes has cerebral palsy and is disabled. She cannot climb stairs or bathe herself. On her doctor's advice and with her landlord's permission, she pays a contractor to install bathroom modifications on the two-story house that she rents. Although the landlord allowed the improvements, he did not pay any of the cost of buying and installing the special accommodations. Which of the following statements is correct?

A. Agnes can deduct the entire amount she paid for the upgrades as a medical expense on Schedule A, subject to AGI limitations.
B. Agnes cannot deduct any of the expenses as a medical expense because she does not own the home.
C. Agnes cannot deduct any of the expenses because none were for the treatment of her medical condition.
D. Agnes can deduct a portion of the expenses as an adjustment to income on Form 1040.

56. Dahlia is a tax preparer who reports her business income on Schedule C. She prepares the tax return for Biotex Services, Inc. and charges the company $1,800 for the tax return preparation and bookkeeping. Biotex Services, Inc. is having financial difficulties, so the company offers Dahlia a laptop worth $2,000 in lieu of paying the debt. Dahlia agrees to accept the computer in full payment of her invoice. How much income would Dahlia report on Schedule C as a result of this transaction?

A. $0
B. $1,800
C. $2,000
D. $3,200

57. Sergio is single and 32. He worked until June 30, and then he lost his job. He sold digital assets (Bitcoin) on August 1 for a $12,000 capital gain. He also had a small amount of interest from municipal bonds. His items of income are listed below. He had no other income or losses for the year. He plans to take the standard deduction. What is Sergio's adjusted gross income on Form 1040?

| Wage income | $42,000 |
| Interest from municipal bonds | $220 |
| Gain from the sale of digital assets (Bitcoin) | $12,000 |

A. $41,780
B. $42,000
C. $54,000
D. $54,220

58. Dustin purchases a condo in Dallas, Texas on August 1, 2023. He lists the property online for short-term rentals. He immediately starts to rent the property. The average rental period is less than seven days. Dustin supplies fresh linens, towels, maid service, and daily continental breakfast to each tenant. On which IRS form should he report this activity on his tax return?

A. Schedule 1.
B. Schedule A.
C. Schedule C.
D. Schedule E.

59. On February 19, 2023, Oliver had a vacation home destroyed by an electrical fire. The house is a total loss. It was not a rental property, but merely a second home. The home originally cost $120,000 ten years ago. It had a Fair Market Value of $320,000 on the date of the casualty. Oliver's insurance company investigated the fire as possible arson, so they did not settle his insurance claim until January 23, 2024, when they paid Oliver $300,000 as an insurance settlement. How long does Oliver have to reinvest the insurance proceeds under the involuntary conversion (Section 1033) rules?

A. February 19, 2024.
B. December 31, 2024.
C. January 23, 2025.
D. December 31, 2026.

60. Which of the following statements is correct regarding the filing of Form 4868, *Application for Automatic Extension of Time to File U.S. Individual Income Tax Return*?

A. A U.S. citizen who is out of the country on vacation on the due date will be allowed an additional twelve months to file when "Out of the Country" is written across the top of Form 4868.
B. Interest is not assessed on any income tax due if Form 4868 is filed.
C. Even though a taxpayer files Form 4868, they will owe interest and may be charged a late payment penalty on the amount owed if the tax is not paid by the regular due date.
D. Form 4868 provides a taxpayer with an automatic six-month extension to file and pay.

61. Sierra Smith died on April 3, 2023. Her estate was valued at $17 million at the time of her death, so the estate has a federal estate tax return filing requirement. When is the Form 706 due for her estate?

A. October 15, 2023
B. October 3, 2024
C. April 15, 2024
D. January 3, 2024

62. Which of the following is NOT a deductible medical expense?

A. Travel expenses related to medical care.
B. Birth control pills.
C. Maternity clothing.
D. Vasectomy.

63. Bowen and Marguerite are married and file jointly. They owned and lived in a home as their primary residence for over 15 years. They had purchased it for $273,000 and sold it for $805,000 on February 9, 2023. In the same year, the couple sold their Maui vacation condo, which they had purchased for $195,000 13 months ago. They sold the condo at a loss for $191,000 on April 5, 2023. What amounts of taxable gain (or loss) result from these two real estate transactions?

A. $0 taxable gain; $4,000 of capital loss.
B. $32,000 of long-term capital gain.
C. $32,000 of capital gain; $4,000 of ordinary loss.
D. $529,000 of long-term capital gain.

64. Beatrix purchased 500 shares of Wolfram Graphics, Inc. stock on February 2, 2023. She paid $11,000 for all the shares. On December 12, 2023, she received 50 additional shares as a nontaxable stock dividend. What is her new basis *per share* at the end of the year?

A. $10 per share.
B. $20 per share.
C. $22 per share.
D. $24 per share.

65. Jarome is age 27 and unmarried. He does not have any dependents. In 2022 (the prior year), he earned $8,700 in wages and had no other income. He did not have to pay income tax because his gross income was less than the filing requirement. He filed a return only to have his withheld income tax refunded to him. In 2023, Jarome began to work as a self-employed plumber. He expects to earn $30,000 in 2023. Based on his income and expenses, Jarome expects his tax liability for the year to be $3,684. Jarome made no estimated tax payments during the year. Will he owe an underpayment penalty for failure to pay estimated tax?

A. He will owe an underpayment penalty.
B. He will owe a failure-to-pay penalty, not an underpayment penalty.
C. He will owe an underpayment penalty, but only for amounts owed over $1,000.
D. He will not owe an underpayment penalty as long as he files and pays before the unextended due date.

66. Orson buys a residential rental property on May 25, 2023. He pays the seller $35,000 in cash and assumes the seller's existing mortgage of $81,000 on the property. He also pays $1,300 in legal fees to close the deal. There was also an additional $800 charge for an appraisal required by the lender. Based on this information, what is Orson's adjusted basis in the property?

A. $35,000
B. $115,000
C. $117,300
D. $118,100

67. Which of the following types of income is not "qualifying income" for the purposes of the Earned Income Tax Credit?

A. Nontaxable combat pay.
B. Union strike benefits.
C. Jury duty pay.
D. Income from casual gambling.

68. Trent is a high school science teacher. He spent $800 of his own money on books, computer software, and other supplementary materials for his classroom in 2023. His wife, Aleksandra, is an adjunct professor at a local community college. She spent $220 of her own money on books and other supplies for the courses she teaches. They are both full-time teachers. The couple files jointly. What amount can they claim for an educator expense deduction in 2023?

A. $250
B. $300
C. $470
D. $600

69. Hayley and Hank are not married, but they have a 9-year-old daughter together, named Brianne. Hayley and Hank do not live together, and Brianne lives with her mother most of the week and only stays with her father on weekends. Hank earned $79,000 in wages during the year. Hayley earned $22,000 in wages. Both parents support Brianne, but since Hank earns more, he helps Hayley out with her living expenses. Hank pays Hayley's rent and over half the cost of the apartment where his daughter lives. He also paid $4,000 for Brianne's daycare in 2023. Can Hank file as Head of Household and claim the Child and Dependent Care Credit?

A. Hank cannot claim the Dependent Care Credit, and he cannot file as Head of Household.
B. Hank can file as Head of Household, but he cannot claim the credit for dependent care.
C. Hank cannot file as Head of Household, but he is allowed to claim the dependent care credit.
D. Hank can file as Head of Household, and he can claim the credit for dependent care.

70. Felix and Natasha are married but file separately (MFS). They do not live together, but have no plans to divorce. In 2023, Felix sells 300 shares of Stearns Company stock for a ($4,000) long-term capital loss. He has no other capital gains or losses. Fifteen days after Felix sells his stock, Natasha purchases 500 shares of stock in Stearns Company. How should the stock sale be reported on Felix's separate tax return?

A. Felix can deduct the $4,000 on his tax return as a long-term capital loss.
B. Felix can deduct $3,000 of the loss on his tax return, and the remaining $1,000 must be carried over to the next year.
C. Felix can deduct $1,500 of the loss on his tax return, and the remaining $2,500 must be carried over to the next year.
D. Felix has a wash sale, and he cannot deduct the loss.

71. Sherry died on September 1, 2023. At the time of her death, she had the following assets:

| Roth IRA | $150,000 |
| --- | --- |
| Undeveloped land titled in her name | $15,000 |
| Life insurance proceeds payable to her children | $1,750,000 |
| Brokerage account held jointly with her spouse | $1,100,000 |
| Checking account held in her name only | $30,000 |
| Vacation home held jointly with her spouse | $500,000 |

Sherry also had $50,000 of outstanding medical bills at the time of her death. Her husband, who is also the executor of her estate, paid the outstanding medical bills on January 9, 2024 (the following year). Sherry's husband plans to file an estate tax return in order to make a portability election. What is the amount of her *gross estate* on Form 706?

A. $2,545,000
B. $2,695,000
C. $2,745,000
D. $3,545,000

72. Cadence is 40 and files MFS. She has lived apart from her husband for three years, but they are not legally separated or divorced. Her modified AGI was $139,000 in 2023. Is she allowed to contribute to a Roth IRA?

A. Yes, she can contribute to a Roth, and her contribution is not limited.
B. No, she cannot contribute to a Roth because her income is too high.
C. Yes, she can contribute to a Roth, but her contribution is limited by her MAGI.
D. No, she cannot contribute to a Roth because she is filing MFS.

73. Which of the following types of income is taxable to the recipient?

A. Damage awards for physical injury or sickness.
B. Traditional IRA distributions to a beneficiary after the death of the original account owner.
C. Accelerated death benefits for a terminally ill individual under a life insurance contract.
D. Municipal bond interest.

74. Angela and Hernan are married and file jointly. On August 13, 2023, Hernan dies. Angela does not remarry before the end of the year. Angela and Hernan have one child, a 12-year-old son, who now lives with Angela. For filing status purposes, the IRS considers Angela to have been _____ all year.

A. Married
B. Unmarried
C. Single
D. Widowed

75. Braxton is having money troubles and agrees to sell his condo to Aimee. Aimee pays $224,000 in cash for the home and also agrees to pay all of Braxton's delinquent real estate taxes on the residence, totaling $1,900. How must Aimee treat the property tax payment of $1,900?

A. The taxes can be prorated and deducted over the life of her loan.
B. Aimee cannot deduct the taxes. Instead, she must add the taxes to her basis in the property.
C. Aimee can deduct the property taxes as an itemized deduction on her Schedule A.
D. Aimee can deduct the property taxes as a business expense on Schedule C.

76. Azumi is single and does not receive any tax credits. She works as an employee and earns regular wages. Her wages didn't increase in 2023, but she won a $9,000 cash prize that increased her AGI. She wants to avoid paying an estimated tax penalty. Based on the amounts listed below, is Azumi required to pay estimated tax in the current year?

| AGI for the prior year (wages only) | $73,700 |
|---|---|
| Total tax on prior-year return | $9,224 |
| Anticipated AGI for the current year (wages plus + $9,000 cash prize) | $82,700 |
| Total current year estimated tax | $11,270 |
| **Tax expected to be withheld from her wages in the current year** | **$10,250** |

A. No, she is not required to make estimated tax payments.
B. Yes, she is required to make estimated tax payments if she wants to avoid a penalty.
C. She is not required to make estimated payments, but she must increase her withholding at her job.
D. None of the above is correct.

77. None of the individuals listed below are U.S. citizens, and none of them have a U.S. green card. However, all of them have U.S.-source income. Which of the following individuals is considered *exempt* for purposes of the substantial presence test?

A. Salem, who is temporarily in the United States as a college instructor on a J-1 visa.
B. Fumiko, an undocumented alien who is present in the United States without a valid visa.
C. Christian, a professional golf player temporarily in the United States to play in a tournament.
D. All of the individuals listed are subject to the substantial presence test.

78. Regina owns a clothing store in Reno, Nevada, which she operates as a sole proprietorship. She collects sales tax on behalf of each customer's purchase, as Nevada imposes a sales tax on the buyer of physical goods. Regina is required to collect and remit the sales tax on behalf of the state. Which of the following is a correct statement about the sales tax Regina collects from her customers in connection with the sale of products?

A. Sales taxes collected are considered taxable income until the taxes are remitted to the taxing authorities.
B. The sales taxes collected are deducted from her gross receipts.
C. The sales taxes collected are added to her gross receipts.
D. The sales taxes collected are excluded from her gross receipts and deductible expenses.

79. Amy received the following income during the year:

| Source | Taxable? |
|---|---|
| Wages | $26,200 |
| Interest income | $5,400 |
| Child support payments | $6,200 |
| Taxable alimony income (her divorce was finalized in 2017) | $7,400 |
| Inheritance from her deceased brother | $12,600 |
| Worker's compensation | $2,300 |
| Hobby income from selling two paintings | $5,300 |

Based on the amounts above, what is Amy's gross income before any adjustments and deductions are applied?

A. $41,300
B. $44,300
C. $52,800
D. $63,100

80. Vincent's adjusted gross income is $45,000 in 2023. He has $8,000 in qualifying medical expenses during the year. Vincent also pays an additional $2,000 in medical expenses for his daughter, Luanne, who is 10 years old, but does not live with him. He does not claim his daughter as a dependent on his tax return, because his ex-wife is the custodial parent. Vincent chooses to itemize his deductions this year. What is his allowable deduction for medical expenses on Schedule A?

A. $3,375
B. $4,625
C. $6,625
D. $6,825

81. Zoe was an attorney and a 10% partner in Goldwin Attorneys, LLP. The partnership reports its income on a calendar year. Zoe dies on July 31, 2023, and her partnership interest passes to her estate. The distributive share of partnership income allocable to Zoe's interest through the date of her death was $70,000 (for the entire year, it was $120,000). How should the distributive partnership income be reported, based on Zoe's partnership interest?

A. $70,000 will be reported on Zoe's final return (Form 1040); $120,000 will be reported on Form 1041.
B. $120,000 will be reported on Zoe's final tax return (Form 1040).
C. $70,000 will be reported on Zoe's final tax return (Form 1040), $50,000 will be reported on Form 1041.
D. $120,000 will be reported on Form 1041.

82. Which of the following taxpayers is the most likely to be required to pay estimated taxes?

A. A household employee.
B. A nonresident alien with U.S. investments who is subject to backup withholding.
C. A statutory employee.
D. A statutory nonemployee.

83. Ayden is single and 36 years old. He is a U.S. citizen who lives and works overseas. He has no dependents. In 2023, he earns $98,000 in wages in Spain. He has no U.S.-based income and no itemized deductions. Ayden should file using which tax form?

A. Form 1040-NR.
B. Form 1040-SR.
C. Form 1040.
D. Ayden does not have to file, because he qualifies for the Foreign Earned Income Exclusion.

84. Sybil, a U.S. citizen, lives and works in Ireland. Her income included $80,000 in wages from her Irish employer, $200 in interest from a U.S. bank, $500 in online gambling winnings, and $7,000 in child support payments from her ex-spouse. She also had $8,000 in gambling losses for the year. What is her gross income (before the calculation of any exclusions or credits)?

A. $700
B. $79,700
C. $80,700
D. $87,500

85. Anton is unmarried and age 68. He does not have any dependents. On May 20, 2023, Anton wins $16,000 at a casino. The casino withholds $1,300 in federal income taxes on the winnings. He also has $18,500 in gambling losses in 2023. Anton itemizes deductions. He is not a professional gambler. How should this be reported on his return?

A. Anton must report $16,000 of gambling winnings as "other income." He should also report the $1,300 withholding on his return. He cannot deduct any of his gambling losses.
B. Anton must report $16,000 of gambling winnings as "other income." He should also report the $1,300 withholding on his return. Anton can deduct $18,500 in gambling losses as an itemized deduction on Schedule A.
C. Anton should report his net gambling losses of $2,500 ($18,500 - $16,000) as "other income." He should also report the $1,300 withholding on his return.
D. Anton must report $16,000 of gambling winnings. He should also report the $1,300 withholding on his return. Anton can deduct up to $16,000 of gambling losses as an itemized deduction on Schedule A.

86. Deacon has three kids in college. They are all his dependents:

1. Brianna, age 21, a college sophomore working on her first bachelor's degree.
2. Devon, age 19, a college freshman working on his first bachelor's degree.
3. Keisha, age 23, a college graduate working on her first master's degree after having completed and graduated from a four-year undergraduate program.

Based on the above scenario, what is the *maximum* amount of American Opportunity Tax Credits (AOTC) Deacon can potentially claim on his tax return?

A. $2,500
B. $5,000
C. $6,500
D. $7,500

87. Tamara and Garfield are married and file jointly in a non-community property state. In 2023, they decide to give Tamara's nephew, Jared, $28,000. Garfield writes a single check to Jared. Tamara and Garfield both consent to the gift. What are the tax consequences of this gift?

A. The gift is taxable to Jared on his individual return.
B. The gift is taxable to Tamara and Garfield on their joint return.
C. The gift is not taxable, but it must be reported on Form 709.
D. The gift is neither taxable nor reportable on Form 709.

88. U.S. Armed Forces personnel and retirees receive many different types of pay and allowances. Which of the following types of income is taxable?

A. Qualified hazardous duty pay.
B. Military severance pay.
C. Basic Allowance for Housing (BAH).
D. VA disability compensation.

89. In 2023, Edith gave the following gifts:

- $36,000 for her grandson Callan's tuition, which was paid directly to the college.
- $18,000 to her brother, Johan.
- $19,000 donation to the Libertarian Party (not a qualifying charity).
- $15,000 to her cousin, Abigail.
- $22,000 to her church.

How should these gifts be reported under the gift tax rules?

A. Edith does not need to file any gift tax returns.
B. Edith must file a gift tax return and report all the gifts.
C. Edith must file a gift tax return and report Callan's gift and Johan's gift.
D. Edith must file a gift tax return and report the $18,000 gift to her brother Johan.

90. Hassan is 42 and single. He works full-time for Innova Laboratories, Inc. and earns $200,000 in wages as an engineer. He has a second job as a consultant where he earns $40,000 in wages. Lastly, he has $22,000 in interest income from a certificate of deposit. What is Hassan's Additional Medicare Tax (the threshold for single taxpayers is $200,000)?

A. $0
B. $160
C. $360
D. $2,358

91. What type of income is typically reported as "other income" on Schedule 1 of Form 1040?

A. Rental income.
B. Capital gains and losses.
C. Farming income or (loss).
D. Lottery winnings.

92. Gunnar files as head of household and has one dependent child. In 2023, Gunnar had a modified adjusted gross income of $45,000 and the following medical expenses:

| Type of Expense | Cost |
|---|---|
| Inpatient treatment for drug addiction | $4,995 |
| Dental procedures | $405 |
| Acid reflux pills (prescription) | $75 |
| Childcare incurred while visiting a physician | $312 |
| Hair transplant surgery | $5,500 |

What is his allowable medical expense deduction on Schedule A *after* applying the AGI limitations?

A. $2,100
B. $3,375
C. $4,380
D. $5,475

93. Letty works as a receptionist during the week and part-time as a waitress on the weekends. Based on the amounts below, what will Letty report as taxable wage income on her individual Form 1040?

| | |
|---|---|
| Receptionist, Form W-2 wages | $25,600 |
| Waitress, Form W-2 wages | $4,950 |
| Waitress, unreported tips | $300 |
| Unemployment compensation | $3,700 |
| State income tax refund | $2,000 |

A. $30,550
B. $30,850
C. $34,250
D. $36,550

94. Foster is 27 years old and a full-time college student, working on his first bachelor's degree. He is attending a junior college and paid $2,000 in qualifying educational expenses in 2023. He plans to claim the American Opportunity Tax Credit (AOTC) on his return. What is the maximum amount of AOTC that he is eligible for?

A. 25% of $2,000 in qualifying expenses.
B. 50% of $2,000 in qualifying expenses.
C. 75% of $2,000 in qualifying expenses.
D. 100% of $2,000 in qualifying expenses.

95. Nathaniel is age 57 and unmarried. He has one adult daughter named Desiree. On May 12, 2023, Nathaniel dies. His final will names his daughter, Desiree, as his executor and the sole beneficiary of his estate. Nathaniel's gross estate is valued at $18 million on the date of his death. Desiree compiles the following list of expenses and losses related to her late father's estate:

| Funeral and burial costs | $23,000 |
| Attorney's fees related to the estate | $37,950 |
| Credit card debts owed at the time of death | $86,500 |
| Unpaid mortgage on the decedent's primary residence | $723,700 |
| Property taxes accrued after death | $26,000 |

Based on the amounts listed above, what is the amount deductible against the gross estate for Estate Tax purposes?

A. $124,450
B. $871,150
C. $874,150
D. $897,150

96. Theodore married Sydney three years ago. They have always filed their taxes jointly. In March 2023, Theodore discovers that Sydney was married before, and never properly divorced from her first husband. Theodore moves out in November and hires an attorney who files for an annulment under the charge of bigamy. Theodore's annulment is granted on February 2, 2024. Theodore does not have any children or dependents. Under these circumstances, what is Theodore's filing status for the 2023 tax year?

A. Married Filing Jointly.
B. Married Filing Separately.
C. Head of Household.
D. Single.

97. In 2023, Jaxson had a number of stock dispositions. His investment transactions were:

| Activity | Bought | Sold |
|---|---|---|
| Sold 1,400 shares of Depot, Inc. stock for $3,000 (basis: $1,400) | 1/3/2020 | 12/1/2023 |
| Sold 200 shares of Lection, Inc. for $500 (basis: $1,000) | 1/3/2017 | 12/25/2023 |
| Sold 50 shares of Hibbert, Inc. stock for $1,700 (basis: $1,500) | 2/1/2023 | 9/12/2023 |

Based on all the transactions listed above, what is Jaxson's net long-term capital gain (or loss)?

A. $1,000 long-term capital loss.
B. $1,100 long-term capital gain.
C. $1,200 long-term capital gain.
D. $1,600 long-term capital gain.

98. Naomi is 29 years old and single. She is not a student and does not have any dependents. She has an AGI of $27,000, all from wages. Naomi contributed $1,500 to her employer-sponsored 401(k) during the tax year. Which credit might she be eligible for on her 2023 tax return?

A. Child and Dependent Care Credit.
B. Credit for Other Dependents.
C. Earned Income Tax Credit.
D. Retirement Savings Contributions Credit.

99. Kendra is unmarried and earned $175,000 in wages for the year. She also has $22,000 of passive income from a limited partnership, and a $24,000 loss from rental real estate activities in which she actively participated. She is not a real estate professional. How should these activities be treated on her individual tax return?

A. She can use $22,000 of passive income from the partnership investment to offset $22,000 of her rental loss. The remaining rental losses of $2,000 would be deductible from her wages.
B. She must recognize $22,000 of passive income from the partnership. All the rental losses must be carried over because her wages exceed the phaseout threshold of $100,000.
C. She can use $22,000 of passive income from the partnership investment to offset $22,000 of her rental loss. The remaining rental losses of $2,000 would be deductible on Schedule A as a miscellaneous itemized deduction.
D. She can use $22,000 of passive income from the partnership investment to offset $22,000 of her rental loss. The remaining rental losses of $2,000 ($22,000 - $24,000) would need to be carried over to the following year.

100. Slade and Maeve are married and file jointly. They are both aged 59. They both work part-time jobs, and their 2023 combined adjusted gross income is $39,900. Slade contributes $1,800 to his traditional IRA plan during the year. Maeve contributes $1,000 to her Roth IRA. They are eligible for a Retirement Savings Contribution Credit of 50%. What is the dollar amount of their credit on their MFJ return?

A. $500
B. $1,000
C. $1,400
D. $2,000

**Please review your answer choices with the correct answers in the next section.**

# Answers to Exam #1: Individuals

**1. The answer is C.** William may deduct his own HSA contributions on his Form 1040 (via Form 8889 and Schedule 1) as an adjustment to income. A health savings account (HSA) is a tax-favored medical savings account available to taxpayers. HSAs are owned by individuals, but contributions may be made by an employer, the taxpayer themselves, or any other person. Amounts in an HSA may be accumulated over the years and distributed on a tax-free basis to pay for or reimburse qualified medical expenses. The HSA contribution limit (employer + employee) for 2023 is $3,850 for a single individual, so he did not make an overcontribution.

**Note**: If a taxpayer makes cash deposits directly into their own health savings account (HSA), they can take an HSA tax deduction on their individual tax return. Generally, HSA contributions paid through an employer are already excluded from taxable income on the employee's W-2. If a taxpayer uses the health savings account (HSA) to pay medical expenses, then they cannot itemize medical deductions for the same expenses (no "double-dipping"). However, if the taxpayer has additional medical expenses that are not paid with HSA funds, they may be able to claim those additional expenses as an itemized deduction on Schedule A.

**2. The answer is B.** Because of his age and filing status, Akram does not have to file a return in 2023. The gross income filing threshold for head of household for those under 65 is $20,800 in 2023, but $22,650 for those 65 or older. Since Akram is 65, he is not required to file a return. However, he may still choose to file to receive any refunds or credits that he may qualify for.

**3. The answer is C.** All of Clayton's bookkeeping-related income is taxable as self-employment income. Clayton must report $22,400 + $2,500 ($24,900) as self-employment income on his Schedule C. Therefore, this income is subject to income tax, as well as self-employment tax. The fees Clayton received for services performed as a notary public ($250) are subject to income tax, but not self-employment tax. For more information on this topic, see the IRS instructions for *Schedule SE*.

**4. The answer is C.** Jacob cannot deduct any expenses associated with the cycling competitions, but he must claim any prizes as income, as his cycling will likely have to be classified as a hobby. Costs related to a hobby activity are no longer deductible due to the suspension of miscellaneous itemized deductions by the *Tax Cuts and Jobs Act (TCJA)*. The IRS is likely to determine that Jacob is engaging in a "hobby" because the cycling competitions are not engaged in for profit. Although he maintains adequate records and enters the competitions with the ability to earn money, he continues to enter competitions despite sustaining losses over several years, suggesting the lack of a true profit motive. A "hobby" is an activity typically undertaken primarily for pleasure. The IRS presumes that an activity is "carried on for a profit" if it makes a profit during at least three of the last five tax years, including the current year.

**5. The answer is B.** Only the jury duty pay would be reported as "other income" on Schedule 1 of Janelle's Form 1040. Jury duty pay is typically reported to the juror on a 1099-MISC only if the amount totals $600 or more, but any amount received is taxable. The other sources of income are fully taxable, but not reported on Schedule 1. The rental income would generally be reported on Schedule E, and the Social Security income and wages would be reported directly on Page 1 of Form 1040.

**6. The answer is C.** The cost of the first $50,000 of life insurance coverage is excludable; the cost of the remaining $90,000 in coverage is taxable to Evie as wages. An employer can exclude the cost of the first $50,000 of group-term life insurance coverage provided under a policy carried directly or indirectly by an employer. The imputed cost of coverage in excess of $50,000 must be included in the employee's income and subject to employment taxes. If the optional policy was not considered "carried by the employer," none of the $100,000 optional coverage would be included in the employee's income. Group-term life insurance that exceeds $50,000 of coverage is subject to Social Security and Medicare taxes, but not FUTA tax or income tax withholding, even when provided as a qualified benefit in a cafeteria plan. For more information on this topic, see Publication 15-A, *Employer's Supplemental Tax Guide.*

**7. The answer is A.** Vanessa must report the $100 in capital gain distributions. Capital gain distributions, such as those from mutual funds and real estate investment trusts (REITs), are taxable income. These distributions are treated as long-term capital gains, regardless of how long the taxpayer holds the shares. The other types of distributions listed are not taxable. Answer "B" is incorrect because a return of capital reduces a taxpayer's stock basis, and is generally not taxable until a taxpayer's entire basis is recovered. Answer "C" is incorrect because a stock dividend reduces the basis of the individual shares held prior to the distribution. Answer "D" is incorrect because dividends paid to cash-value life insurance policyholders are normally considered nontaxable distributions.

> **Note:** Do not confuse "*capital gains*" with "*capital gain distributions.*" A capital gain occurs when a taxpayer sells stock, shares of a mutual fund, or another capital asset. A capital gain distribution occurs when the mutual fund sells assets for more than their cost and distributes the realized gain to its investors.

**8. The answer is A.** Corwin can deduct the penalty as an adjustment to income on Schedule 1 of Form 1040. This type of penalty applies when a depositor withdraws funds before a time deposit account matures. Taxpayers can adjust their income by deducting penalties they paid for withdrawing funds from a deferred interest account before maturity. A penalty for early withdrawal of funds from a savings account may be charged when the depositor withdraws funds before the maturity date for a time deposit (also called a "certificate of deposit" or "CD").

**9. The answer is B.** Nadia and Jasmine will be treated as each having received $9,000 of rental income ($18,000 × 50%) and $6,000 of taxable interest ($12,000 × 50%) as the entire amount of DNI ($30,000) was distributed during the year. They would report the income on Schedule E of their Form 1040. An amount distributed to a beneficiary retains the same character for the beneficiary that it had for the estate (this question is based on an example in Publication 559).

**10. The answer is D.** Filing status is based in part on the taxpayer's marital status on the last day of the tax year. Therefore, Jason would be considered unmarried for tax purposes, because he was legally divorced before the end of the year. Answer "B" is incorrect because in the case of a widowed taxpayer, if a taxpayer's spouse died during the year and the surviving spouse did not remarry, then the surviving spouse is still considered "married" for tax purposes and can file jointly with their deceased spouse.

**11. The answer is D.** Simon cannot claim Allie as a dependent because Allie is Simon's live-in housekeeper. Household employees can never be claimed as dependents. Household employees include housekeepers, maids, babysitters, gardeners, and others who work in or around a taxpayer's private residence.

**12. The answer is C.** Because of changes in the Tax Cuts and Jobs Act, unreimbursed employee expenses are no longer deductible for *most* taxpayers. However, some employees are still permitted to use Form 2106 to deduct their unreimbursed employee expenses on their federal returns. Form 2106 may be used only by the following employees:

- Armed Forces reservists.
- Qualified performing artists.
- Fee-basis state or local government officials.
- Disabled employees with impairment-related work expenses.

Due to the suspension of miscellaneous itemized deductions subject to the 2% floor, employees who do not fit into one of the listed categories above may not use Form 2106 to deduct their unreimbursed employee expenses.

**13. The answer is B.** The basis of property received from a decedent's estate is generally the fair market value of the property on the date of the decedent's death. However, when an executor elects the *alternate valuation date*, the basis to the heirs is generally the fair market value of the assets six months *after* the date of death. Only if assets are distributed *prior* to six months after the date of death will the basis to the heirs be the fair market value of the assets as of the date of distribution. In this case, the stock was distributed to Benjamin *after* the six-month post-death period. Therefore, his basis in the stock is **$21,500**, which is the FMV on August 20 (6 months after the date of his grandmother's death, which is the *alternate valuation date* for the estate). Benjamin's holding period is **long-term**, because inherited property is *always* treated as long-term property, regardless of how long the beneficiary holds the property after he receives it.

**14. The answer is A.** Kamila's standard deduction would be **$13,850** in 2023. In general, the standard deduction for a decedent's final tax return is the same as it would have been had the decedent continued to live. However, if the decedent was not 65 (or older) at the time of death, the *additional* standard deduction for age cannot be claimed. Since Kamila died before she turned 65, she is not eligible for the additional standard deduction on her final return. Kamila's executor would be responsible for filing her final tax return. See IRS *Publication 17* for more information.

**15. The answer is B.** Gina and Anthony must file a joint return to claim the American Opportunity Credit. Qualified education expenses paid on behalf of a student by someone other than the student (such as a spouse or other relative) are treated as paid by the student. In order to take the credit, they would have to file jointly.

**16. The answer is B.** Florencia's maximum deduction on Schedule A for taxes is $10,000. A taxpayer's total *allowable* deduction for state and local income, sales and property taxes is limited to a combined total deduction of $10,000 ($5,000 if Married Filing Separately). Any state and local taxes she paid above this amount cannot be deducted. This is also called the "SALT cap."

**17. The answer is C.** Zachary and Annie have two reporting requirements. They are required to file the FBAR as well as Form 8938. They must file an FBAR directly with the FinCEN using their online FBAR submission website. Form 8938 must be filed with the IRS by the due date (including extensions) of their tax return. Form 8938 is filed along with the taxpayer's Form 1040. The FBAR is filed separately. The FBAR filing due date is *generally* April 15 (to coincide with the due date for individual tax returns). However, an automatic extension is available to October 15 for the FBAR. The extension is automatic, and specific requests for an extension are not required.

**18. The answer is A.** Health insurance for Jeffrey, the owner, is not deductible on Schedule C. Health insurance for a sole proprietor, subject to self-employment income requirements, is deductible, but not on Schedule C. Instead, it is claimed as an adjustment to income on Schedule 1 of Form 1040. For self-employed individuals filing Schedule C or Schedule F, the insurance policy can be either in the name of the business or in the name of the individual. Other types of insurance, including any health insurance costs paid on behalf of employees, would be deductible as ordinary business expenses on Schedule C.

**19. The answer is B.** Individuals who have been physically present for at least **183 days** over a three-year period, including the current year, meet the requirements of the substantial presence test and will be taxed as a resident of the U.S. The substantial presence test requirements include 183 days of physical presence over a three-year period comprising the current year (must be at least 31 days); the first year before the current year (where each day present in the U.S. is counted as one-third of a day); and the second year before the current year (where each day present in the U.S. is counted as one-sixth of a day).

**20. The answer is D.** The entire gain can be excluded from income. Stetson meets the ownership and use tests to exclude the gain because he owned and lived in the home for more than two years during the five-year period ending on the date of sale, so he can exclude up to $250,000 of gain from the sale of the home as a single individual. The required two years of ownership and use do not have to be continuous, nor do they have to occur at the same time. A taxpayer will meet the tests if he can show that he owned and lived in the property as a primary residence for either 24 full months or 730 days (365 × 2) during the five-year period ending on the date of sale.

**21. The answer is A.** A taxpayer's "tax home" is usually determined by the location of his principal place of *work*, regardless of his mailing address or where he actually lives. So, Donnie's "tax home" would be in Texas, the location of his principal place of work (where his business is located). A taxpayer's "tax home" is used for tax purposes, including determining if travel expenses are deductible.

**22. The answer is C.** Jerry can deduct $50,000 in ordinary losses on his individual tax return. Special rules apply to Section 1244 stocks, which allow a shareholder to deduct their losses on the stock as an ordinary loss, up to $50,000 (or $100,000 if married filing jointly), instead of treating the losses as capital losses, which are subject to $3,000 limit ($1,500 if married filing separately).

**23. The answer is A.** Tatum may deduct the entire cost of the fire protection system using Section 179. Since Tatum's building is a commercial building (not a residential rental), then the cost of the fire protection system would qualify. There are certain types of improvement property eligible for Section 179 that can potentially be immediately deducted if the costs are incurred on *nonresidential* real property. These are:

- Nonresidential roofs
- Heating, ventilation, and air-conditioning property (HVAC systems)
- Fire protection and alarm systems
- Security systems

**24. The answer is B.** Abiram may deduct his charitable contributions to U.S. nonprofit organizations only. Nonresident aliens are allowed to deduct certain itemized deductions on their Forms 1040-NR. For more information, see Publication 519, *U.S. Tax Guide for Aliens.*

**25. The answer is B.** Form 8938 requires U.S. persons to report various types of assets, not just bank accounts. These assets include, but are not limited to, foreign financial accounts, foreign securities, interests in foreign entities, and any financial instrument or contract with an issuer or counterparty that is not a U.S. person.

**26. The answer is C.** Kerrie is eligible for the Premium Tax Credit from January through July, assuming she meets all the eligibility criteria. The Premium Tax Credit (PTC) is a refundable tax credit for health insurance purchased through the Health Insurance Marketplace. To be eligible for the Premium Tax Credit, the taxpayer must have been enrolled at some point during the year in one or more qualified health plans offered through the Health Insurance Marketplace (both federal and state exchanges qualify). For more information, see Publication 974, *Premium Tax Credit*.

**27. The answer is B.** Mai-Lin can deduct only **$15,000** ($25,000 - [50% × $20,000]) of the rental losses in the current year. Taxpayers (other than real estate professionals) who actively participate in a rental real estate activity can deduct up to $25,000 of loss from the activity from nonpassive income. However, the $25,000 allowance is phased out if modified adjusted gross income (MAGI) is between $100,000 and $150,000. The $25,000 maximum deduction gets phased out by $1 for every $2 that the taxpayer's MAGI is over $100,000. If the taxpayer's MAGI is $150,000 or more ($75,000 or more if married filing separately), then no deduction can be claimed for a rental activity loss for the year. Generally, any disallowed losses will be carried forward to subsequent years until absorbed by profits, or other income. This unique "rental loss" allowance is an exception to the general rule disallowing passive losses in excess of income from passive activities. For more information, see Publication 527, *Residential Rental Property*.

**28. The answer is D.** Tristan meets the requirements to file as a Qualifying Surviving Spouse (QSS). The Qualifying Surviving Spouse (QSS) filing status is available to the taxpayer for two years *after* the year of the spouse's death. A surviving spouse may choose to file jointly with his deceased spouse in the year of death. Then, in the two subsequent years, the surviving spouse may use the Qualifying Surviving Spouse (QSS) filing status, provided that they have a qualifying dependent.

**29. The answer is B.** On Royce's tax return, he can deduct up to $3,000 of the capital loss. The unused part of the loss, $4,000 ($7,000 - $3,000), can be carried over to the following year. Royce's adjusted gross income is **$49,000** ($52,000 - $3,000 capital loss). Capital losses can be deducted on a taxpayer's return and used to reduce other income, such as wages, up to an annual limit of $3,000 (or $1,500 if MFS).

> **Note:** Excess capital losses will carry forward indefinitely during a taxpayer's life. However, they do not transfer after death. If a taxpayer dies with a capital loss carryover, the unused losses do not transfer to a surviving spouse or to the deceased taxpayer's estate.

**30. The answer is A.** The Additional Medicare Tax of 0.9% is applied only to *earned* income ($188,000 + $10,000 + $56,000 = $254,000) above the threshold for a taxpayer's filing status. Therefore, Dennis owes **$486** ($254,000 - $200,000 = $54,000 × .009 = $486). The interest income and the inheritance do not figure into the calculation because interest income is unearned income, and the inheritance is not taxable. This tax is reported on Form 8959.

**31. The answer is A.** An IRA participant who misses the 60-day rollover window may be eligible for an automatic waiver of the 60-day rollover rule if certain requirements are met. Because the error was committed by her financial institution, Dixie may request an automatic waiver of the 60-day rollover requirement. The taxpayer can also request and receive a private letter ruling (PLR) granting a waiver of the 60-day rollover requirement. The IRS permits an automatic waiver of the sixty-day rollover period for retirement plan distributions under 11 common circumstances (usually where the financial institution is at fault for not properly rolling over the funds).

> **Note:** There is no fee for using the "self-certification" procedure. Dixie can also request a private letter ruling, but a private letter ruling is not free. The minimum fee for a PLR related to a late IRA rollover is $10,000, so it would behoove Dixie to use the "self-certification" procedure. This procedure is outlined in Revenue Procedure 2016-47.

**32. The answer is C.** Hayato is eligible to take the foreign earned income exclusion based on the physical presence test (see the third bullet point below). For 2023, the maximum exclusion for the foreign earned income exclusion is $120,000. To claim the foreign-earned income exclusion, the foreign housing exclusion, or the foreign housing deduction, the taxpayer must have foreign-earned income, their tax home must be in a foreign country, and they must be ONE of the following:

- A U.S. citizen who is a bona fide resident of a foreign country or countries for an uninterrupted period that includes an entire tax year,
- A U.S. resident alien who is a citizen or national of a country with which the United States has an income tax treaty in effect and who is a bona fide resident of a foreign country or countries for an uninterrupted period that includes an entire tax year, or
- A U.S. citizen or a U.S. resident alien who is physically present in a foreign country or countries for at least 330 full days during any period of 12 consecutive months.

**33. The answer is D.** The Tax Cuts and Jobs Act eliminated the deduction for *most* business-related entertainment expenses, so the tickets to the baseball game are not deductible. Some business meal and entertainment expenses are 100% deductible if the expense is primarily for the benefit of employees who are not highly compensated or key employees. This would include things like a company picnic, holiday party, or a companywide office party. The answer is calculated as follows:

| Expense | Cost | Allowable? | Deduction |
|---|---|---|---|
| Tickets to a baseball game to entertain his client | $196 | NO | $0 |
| Business meal | $78 | 50% in 2023 | $39 |
| A holiday party for Tommy's 12 employees | $560 | 100% deductible | $560 |
| **Allowable deduction** | | | **$599** |

**34. The answer is A.** Phoebe should report the income as wage income. Generally, taxpayers who retire on "FERS" disability must include all of their disability payments in income. These government-related disability payments are taxed as wages until the taxpayer reaches the minimum retirement age (this age is set by the employer). After the taxpayer reaches the minimum retirement age, disability payments are treated as pension income (question modified from an example in Publication 4491).

> **Note:** FERS Disability Retirement is a special benefit awarded to Federal and Postal Service employees that have a physical or mental disability that prevents them from working. Under FERS, the illness or injury does not necessarily need to be related to the job, but often is.

**35. The answer is D.** Since Alfred filed a joint return but is not responsible for the student loan debt, he is entitled to his portion of the refund. He may request his share of the refund by requesting injured spouse relief. He can do this by filing Form 8379, *Injured Spouse Allocation.*

**36. The answer is B.** Katherine may use Head of Household status because she is not married, and she provided over half the cost of keeping up the primary home of her dependent child for more than six months. A taxpayer may still qualify for Head of Household filing status even though the taxpayer is not claiming an exemption for their child if the taxpayer meets the following requirements:

- The taxpayer must be single or "considered unmarried" on the last day of the year.
- The taxpayer paid more than half of the cost of keeping up a home, which was the main home of their child for more than half of the year.

See IRS *Publication 501, Dependents, Standard Deduction, and Filing Information*, for more information.

**37. The answer is C.** Under the "optional method" of calculating the home office deduction, a taxpayer can deduct $5 per square foot for the space in the home that is used for business, with a maximum allowable square footage of 300 square feet. Therefore, the maximum deduction is **$1,500.** The criteria for who qualifies for the deduction remains the same, but the calculation and recordkeeping requirements have been simplified. There is no depreciation expense and no recapture of depreciation upon the sale of the home. Home-related itemized deductions, such as for mortgage interest and real estate taxes, may be claimed in full on Schedule A without allocation of portions to the home office space.

**38. The answer is C.** Rental income is typically reported on Schedule E and is not subject to self-employment tax. Real estate rental income is generally passive and reported on Schedule E (although there are exceptions). Schedule C is used when the taxpayer provides substantial services to the tenants (such in the case of a hotel, motel, or bed and breakfast), or if the rental is part of a trade or business as a bona-fide real estate dealer.

**39. The answer is D.** The expenses paid for an *unsuccessful* adoption attempt in the United States (i.e., a domestic adoption) may still be eligible expenses for the purposes of the Adoption Credit. Qualified adoption expenses include court costs, attorney fees, traveling expenses (including meals and lodging), and other expenses directly related to the legal adoption of an eligible child. Qualified adoption expenses do not include costs for adopting a spouse's child, fees for a surrogate arrangement, or any expenses that were reimbursed by an employer or another organization. Expenses connected with a foreign adoption (in which the child was not a U.S. citizen or U.S. resident at the time the adoption process began) qualify only if the adoption is eventually successful.

**40. The answer is B.** The taxpayer must be a U.S. citizen or legal U.S. resident all year with a Social Security Number that is valid for work purposes. Answer "A" is incorrect because a taxpayer does not need to have a dependent child in order to qualify for the Earned Income Tax Credit. However, the EITC is increased if the taxpayer has a qualifying child. Answer "C" is incorrect because a student can still qualify for EITC if the other tests are met. Answer "D" is incorrect because the Earned Income Credit cannot be claimed by a taxpayer with an ITIN; the taxpayer must have a valid Social Security Number in order to qualify.

**41. The answer is C.** Rohan's basis in the 10 shares received from his father would presumably be his father's adjusted basis, or $100 (this is normally the case, although his basis could also include any gift tax paid by his father related to the appreciation of the stock's value while he held it). Rohan's basis in the stock he purchased would be $620. When shares of stock are sold from lots acquired at different times and the identity of the shares sold cannot be determined, the sale is charged first against the earliest acquisitions (first-in, first-out). The 20 shares sold in October would be presumed to be the 10 shares acquired by gift from Rohan's father and half of the shares he purchased in January. Therefore, the basis of Rohan's Valley Telecom Corporation shares he still owns would be *half* the basis of the purchased shares, or **$310.**

**42. The answer is B.** Piper's qualifying educational costs are determined as follows:

| | |
|---|---|
| Required textbooks | $450 |
| Required lab equipment | $1,260 |
| Tuition ($6,800 - $4,750 scholarship) | $2,050 |
| **Qualifying costs for the AOTC** | **$3,760** |

To figure the amount of qualifying educational expenses for purposes of the AOTC, Piper must first subtract the $4,750 scholarship from tuition expenses ($6,800 - $4,750). The books and lab equipment are allowable expenses, but the student health fees are specifically disallowed (even if they are mandatory). Parking fees or tickets, commuting costs, and meal costs are not allowable for the American Opportunity Tax Credit or the Lifetime Learning Credit.

**43. The answer is A.** Emiko should first contact the payor and attempt to obtain a corrected Form 1099-NEC. For more information, see the IRS instructions for Form 1099-NEC.

**44. The answer is A.** Staci may deduct 100% of the expenses that relate only to the rental portion of the house, and 10% of any qualified expenses that apply to the entire house. When the rental property is a portion of the taxpayer's residence, the rental income and expenses must be allocated separately from the taxpayer's personal expenses. For example, Staci could deduct:

- 100% of the cost to wallpaper the tenant's room, and
- 10% of property taxes, utilities, mortgage interest, and depreciation that apply to the entire home (question modified from an example in Publication 4491).

**45. The answer is B.** Rosalie's ordinary dividends should be reported on Form 1040. Rosalie meets the requirements for reporting the capital gain distribution directly on Form 1040. She does not need a separate form. If a taxpayer's total amount of dividends is *over* $1,500, Schedule B must also be filed with the tax return. Since Rosalie's dividends did not exceed $1,500, Schedule B is not required. The capital gain from the sale of stock should be reported on Schedule D. In some circumstances, the sale of stock may also have to be reported on Form 8949.

**46. The answer is C.** Malika will be forced to file MFS, as a joint return will require both spouses to agree to file jointly and both will need to participate in the preparation and review of the return. She cannot file as head of household because she did not live apart from her husband for the last six months of the year. There is a special exception that applies to married persons who live apart from their spouses for at least the last six months of the year. In this case, the taxpayer will be "considered unmarried" for head of household filing purposes. However, since Anwar and Malika did not separate until August, and they are not legally separated, they are considered *married* for the entire taxable year.

**47. The answer is A.** Life insurance proceeds payable to Dillon's beneficiaries would be included in the calculation of his gross estate. The gross estate includes the value of property that the taxpayer owns at the time of death. In addition to the value of life insurance proceeds, the gross estate includes the following:

- The value of certain annuities payable to the estate or to the taxpayer's heirs, and
- The value of certain property transferred within three years before the taxpayer's death.

Although life insurance proceeds are generally not taxable to the beneficiary who receives them, the value of life insurance proceeds insuring a decedent's life must be included in the valuation of the gross estate if the proceeds are payable to the estate, or to named beneficiaries, if the taxpayer owned the policy at the time of his death.

**48. The answer is B.** Benita should file Form 982 and report the reduction in the basis of her home. The $30,000 in debt cancellation can be excluded as qualified principal residence indebtedness on Form 982 and is not counted as taxable income on her tax return.

**49. The answer is B.** The cleaning deposits are refundable to the tenants, so they are not considered rental income. The advance rent must be included in Kelsey's 2023 rental income. This is because Kelsey had constructive receipt of the rent, and advance rent is always taxable when it is received, regardless of the taxpayer's accounting method. A taxpayer is deemed to have "constructive receipt" of income when the amount is made available without restriction. A taxpayer cannot hold checks or postpone taking possession of income from one tax year to another to avoid paying tax. The fact that Kelsey waited to cash the check is irrelevant because she had rights to the funds. Kelsey must calculate her rental income as follows:

| |
|---|
| $11,700 ($1,300 × 9 months in 2023) |
| $1,800 ($600 × 3 months in 2023) |
| $600 (January rent paid in advance) |
| **$14,100 rental income** |

**50. The answer is D.** Becky has a long-term capital gain of **$370** ($1,320 sale price - $950 transferred basis). The basis of a gift generally remains the same for the gift recipient/donee as it was for the donor when the fair market value of the gifted asset is more than the donor's basis. Therefore, Becky's basis in the stock, for purposes of determining gain, is $950 (transferred basis). The holding period is also transferred, so the five years that Jakob held the stock (before giving it to his daughter) is added to her holding period, which makes the disposition a long-term capital gain when Becky sold it on November 16.

**51. The answer is B.** Chelsea has a taxable gain of $30,000. Her basis in the new rental home is $80,000. The part of her gain that is taxable is $30,000 ($130,000 - $100,000), the unspent portion of the payment from the insurance company that she used to pay down her personal debts. The rest of the gain ($20,000) is not taxable, because it was reinvested into the replacement home. This follows the rules for involuntary conversions (IRC section 1033). The basis of the new home is calculated as follows:

| | |
|---|---|
| Cost of replacement home | $100,000 |
| Subtract gain not recognized | ($20,000) |
| **Basis of the replacement home** | **$80,000** |

**52. The answer is A.** Gains from the sale of personal-use capital assets, such as Aileen's painting, are taxable and must be reported. The auction house's commission is $1,800 ($6,000 × 30%). Therefore, Aileen's taxable gain is **$4,180** ($6,000 - $20 basis - $1,800 commission). The amount is subject to income tax, but not to self-employment tax since it is merely the sale of a personal asset and not business income. She would report the gain on Schedule D as a long-term capital gain. Fine art is considered a "collectible" so the gain would be a long-term capital gain, taxed at ordinary tax rates, but no higher than 28%.

**53. The answer is C.** Only Skye qualifies Serena for the Child Tax Credit in 2023. In 2023, for the purposes of the Child Tax Credit, a "qualifying child" is defined as:

- A son, daughter, stepchild, foster child, brother, sister, stepbrother, stepsister, or a descendant of any of them (for example, a grandchild, niece, or nephew),
- The child must be *under* the age of 17 (age 16 or younger).
- Have not provided over one-half of *their own* support,
- Have lived with the taxpayer for more than half of the year, and
- Be a U.S. citizen, a U.S. national, or a U.S. resident alien.

**54. The answer is A.** Elias had a short-term capital loss of **$1,200.** His basis in the stock sold is figured as follows:

(Gain or Loss = Sales Price - Basis)
($15,000 ÷ 1,000) × 600 shares = $9,000 basis in the shares sold.
Sales Price of 600 shares = $7,800
$7,800 sales price - $9,000 basis = ($1,200)

Since his holding period is less than one year, he has a short-term capital loss of ($1,200). A short-term holding period is a year or less, while a long-term holding period is defined as more than one year (a year *plus* one day or more).

**55. The answer is A.** Agnes can deduct the entire cost as a medical expense on Schedule A (subject to AGI limitations). Amounts paid to buy and install special fixtures for a person with a disability, mainly for medical reasons, in a rented house are deductible medical expenses.

**56. The answer is B.** Dahlia would report $1,800 in business income. Generally, the FMV of property exchanged for services is includable in income. However, if services are performed for a price agreed on beforehand, the amount will be accepted as the FMV if there is no evidence to the contrary.

**57. The answer is C.** Sergio's adjusted gross income is **$54,000** ($42,000 + $12,000). The wages and capital gain from the sale of virtual assets (such as cryptocurrency) are taxable. The municipal bond interest must be reported on the tax return, but it is not taxable and not added to Sergio's taxable income and adjusted gross income.

**58. The answer is C.** Dustin should report the activity on Schedule C, because the average guest stay is fewer than 7 days, and he provides his guests with substantial services. The IRS defines substantial services as daily breakfast or other meals, linen service, regular cleaning, or maid service. This would be similar to a hotel or a bed-and-breakfast. In contrast, the mere furnishing of utilities or cleaning of public areas do not count as substantial services.

**59. The answer is D.** Oliver has until December 31, 2026, to reinvest the proceeds in similar property without having to recognize gain from the involuntary conversion. This is because Oliver first realized a gain from the insurance reimbursement during 2024 (even though the actual fire occurred in 2023), so he will have until December 31, 2026, to replace the property under the involuntary conversion rules. To postpone reporting gain from an involuntary conversion, the taxpayer must buy replacement property within a specified period of time. This is also called the "replacement period." In this case, Oliver's "replacement period" ends two years after the close of the first tax year in which any part of his gain is realized. Since his insurance company did not issue a reimbursement until 2024, the "realized gain" occurs in 2024. As such, Oliver has until the end of 2026 (2 years after the close of the tax year in which the gain is *realized*)[15] to purchase a replacement property. For more information on this topic, see Publication 547, *Casualties, Disasters, and Thefts.*

**60. The answer is C.** The Form 4868 is used to request an extension to file Form 1040. Even though a taxpayer files Form 4868, *Application of Automatic Extension of Time to File U.S. Individual Income Tax Return*, they will owe interest and a late payment penalty on the amount owed if they do not pay the tax owed by the regular due date.

**61. The answer is D.** The estate tax return (Form 706) is generally due nine months after the date of death. Sierra Smith died on April 3, 2023, then IRS Form 706 will be due for her estate on **January 3, 2024**. A six-month extension is available on Form 4768 if requested. The executor of Sierra's estate is responsible for signing and filing the return.

**62. The answer is C.** Maternity clothing is not deductible as a medical expense. Taxpayers can deduct transportation related to medical care. The costs of acupuncture, birth control pills, and permanent sterilization (such as a vasectomy or tubal ligation) are also deductible, even though they may be considered elective, they are expressly permitted. Medical expenses are covered in IRS Publication 502, *Medical and Dental Expenses.*

**63. The answer is B.** Under the section 121 exclusion, Bowen and Marguerite may exclude $500,000 of the gain on their primary residence. They must recognize **$32,000** of long-term capital gain ($805,000 - $273,000 - $500,000 exclusion) in 2023. The exclusion may be claimed only on a main home and not on a second home, and it is subject to both the ownership and use tests. The loss from the Maui vacation home cannot be claimed or netted against the gain from the sale of their primary residence. A loss on a personal residence, regardless of whether it is a main home or a second/vacation home, is not deductible. Therefore, the losses that they incurred on their vacation home would not be reported on their tax return.

---

[15] There are certain events that have a longer replacement period. For example, if the taxpayer has lost property in a Presidentially declared disaster area, the taxpayer has a total of four years in which to replace the lost property.

**64. The answer is B.** Beatrix's original basis per share was $22 ($11,000 cost basis ÷ 500 shares). After the nontaxable stock dividend, her original $11,000 basis would be allocated to the 550 shares (500 original shares plus the 50-share stock dividend). This results in an <u>adjusted basis</u> of **$20 per share** ($11,000 ÷ 550 shares).

**65. The answer is D.** Jarome will not owe an underpayment penalty as long as he files and pays before the unextended due date (this is April 15, 2024, for the current filing season). Even though he will owe tax at the end of the year, Jarome will not incur the underpayment penalty because he had no tax liability in the prior year.

**66. The answer is C.** Orson's adjusted basis in the property is **$117,300.** The answer is calculated as follows: ($35,000 cash + $81,000 mortgage assumption + $1,300 legal fees = $117,300). If a taxpayer buys property and assumes an existing mortgage on the property, the basis includes the amount of the assumed mortgage. The basis also includes the settlement fees and closing costs for buying a property. However, the appraisal costs would not be included in the basis. The following items are examples of settlement fees or closing costs that are included in a property's basis.

- Abstract fees (abstract of title fees).
- Charges for installing utility services.
- Legal fees, settlement costs, and recording fees.
- Transfer taxes.
- Owner's title insurance.
- Any amounts the seller owes that the buyer agrees to pay, such as delinquent property taxes or interest, recording or mortgage fees, charges for improvements or repairs, and sales commissions.

There are costs that the owner cannot include in the basis of the property. The following fees are typical during the purchase of a property, but they cannot be added to the property's basis:

- Casualty insurance premiums.
- Rent for occupancy of the property before closing.
- Charges for utilities or other services related to occupancy of the property before closing.
- Charges connected with getting a loan. The following are examples of these charges:
- Points (discount points, loan origination fees).
- Mortgage insurance premiums.
- Loan assumption fees.
- Cost of a credit report.
- Fees for an appraisal that are required by a lender.
- Fees for refinancing a mortgage.

A taxpayer also cannot include amounts placed in escrow for the *future* payments of items such as taxes and insurance. These costs should not be added to the basis of the property.

**67. The answer is D.** Gambling income does not qualify as "earned income" for purposes of the Earned Income Tax Credit. For purposes of the EITC, earned income includes:

- Wages, salaries, tips, jury duty pay, and union strike benefits
- Long-term disability benefits that are received prior to minimum retirement age
- Statutory employee pay
- Net earnings from self-employment
- Nontaxable combat pay, and
- Qualified Medicaid waiver payments.[16]

**68. The answer is B.** Trent can claim $300 (the maximum amount allowed for 2023) for the educator expense deduction. Aleksandra is not eligible because the deduction is available only for kindergarten through grade 12 teachers, instructors, counselors, principals, and aides who worked at least 900 hours during the year. If Aleksandra had been an eligible educator, she would have been able to claim a deduction for what she spent on supplies. The educator expense deduction is a maximum of $300 per "eligible educator," on a joint return, if both spouses are eligible educators, the couple can claim a maximum deduction of $600 on their jointly-filed return. This deduction is sometimes called the "Teacher Credit."

**69. The answer is A.** Even though Hank provided over half the cost of providing a home for his daughter, he cannot file as Head of Household because his daughter did not live with him for over half the year. He is not eligible for the Child and Dependent Care Credit, either, because only a custodial parent may claim the credit. Hayley cannot be Head of Household either because she did not provide more than one-half the cost of keeping up the home for her daughter. However, as the custodial parent, Haley has the primary right to claim her daughter, Brianne, as her qualifying child. Haley may file as "single."

**70. The answer is D.** Felix has a wash sale, and he cannot deduct the capital loss. A wash sale occurs when a taxpayer sells stock or other securities at a loss and, within 30 days before or after the sale or disposition, the taxpayer buys or acquires substantially identical stock or securities. The wash sale rules also apply if a taxpayer sells stock and then the taxpayer's spouse buys similar stock within 30 days. Since Felix's wife purchased identical securities within 30 days after Felix sold his stock, he has a wash sale. The wash sale rules apply regardless of whether the spouses file separate tax returns. Felix's unrecognized $4,000 loss is added to the cost basis of the new stock (the 500 shares of Stearns Company that was purchased 15 days after the sale). The result is an increased basis in the new stock. This adjustment postpones the loss deduction until the disposition of the new stock or securities. The holding period for the new stock includes the holding period of the stock or securities sold.

---

[16] Although combat pay and qualified Medicare waiver payments are generally not taxable, the taxpayer can elect to have this income included in income for the Earned Income Tax Credit if it gives them a better tax result.

**71. The answer is C.** The calculation of Sherry's gross estate includes all of the assets she owned outright at the date of her death, including the life insurance proceeds payable to her beneficiaries. However, only half of the amounts of the assets she owned jointly with her husband would be included in the calculation. Therefore, the answer is figured as follows:

| Asset | Value | % Included | Amount |
|---|---|---|---|
| Roth IRA | $150,000 | 100% | $150,000 |
| Undeveloped land | $15,000 | 100% | $15,000 |
| Life insurance payable to her children | $1,750,000 | 100% | $1,750,000 |
| Brokerage account held jointly | $1,100,000 | 50% | $550,000 |
| Checking account held in her name only | $30,000 | 100% | $30,000 |
| Vacation home held jointly with her spouse | $500,000 | 50% | $250,000 |
| **Value of Sherry's Gross Estate** | | | **$2,745,000** |

Calculation: $150,000 IRA + $15,000 land + $1,750,000 life insurance + $30,000 checking account + $550,000 ($1,100,000/2) brokerage account + $250,000 ($500,000/2) other jointly-held property = **$2,745,000.** Debts not paid before the decedent's death, including medical expenses subsequently paid on her behalf, are liabilities that can be deducted from the gross estate on the estate tax return. However, the value of the "gross estate" is figured without regard to these liabilities. Once the executor figures out the value of the gross estate, there are several deductions that are allowable to determine the amount of the *taxable estate*. Medical expenses can also be deducted on the taxpayer's final Form 1040, even if they are paid in the year following the date of death. To make a portability election (also called a "DSUE" election), the decedent's estate must file IRS *Form 706, United States Estate (and Generation-Skipping Transfer) Tax Return.* The election is made by the executor of the deceased spouse's estate. For more information, see Publication 559, *Survivors, Executors, and Administrators.*

**72. The answer is C.** Cadence can contribute to a Roth IRA, but her contribution is subject to a phaseout because of her MAGI (Modified Adjusted Gross Income). Even though Cadence is "married filing separately," she did not live with her spouse at any time during the year, so she may use the higher phase-out threshold for single taxpayers. The 2023 Roth contribution phaseout limits are as follows:

- $138,000 to $153,000 – Single and HOH
- $218,000 to $228,000 – MFJ/QSS
- $0 to $10,000 – Married filing separately (only if lived with spouse)

**73. The answer is B.** Traditional IRA distributions are taxable to the receiver. In the case of a deceased IRA holder, the distribution to the beneficiary is subject to income tax but is not subject to the 10% early withdrawal penalty, regardless of the age of the beneficiary.

**74. The answer is A.** Angela and Hernan are considered "married" all year. If a taxpayer's spouse dies during the year, the surviving spouse is considered *married* for the entire year and can choose either married filing jointly or married filing separately as his or her filing status (assuming the surviving spouse did not remarry during the year).

**75. The answer is B.** Aimee cannot deduct the taxes because they were legally owed by Braxton. Instead, she must add the taxes to her basis in the property. She cannot deduct the delinquent property taxes because she was not the owner of the property when the taxes were imposed. Property taxes paid in connection with a purchase may be added to the buyer's basis if the taxes are for the time period the property was owned by the seller.

**76. The answer is A.** Azumi does not need to pay estimated tax because she expects her current year income tax withholding ($10,250) to be more than her *prior-year* tax of $9,224. Therefore, Azumi qualifies for the safe harbor rule and is not required to make estimated tax payments. Her expected income tax withholding is also more than 90% of the expected tax liability on her current year return ($11,270 × 90% = $10,143). A taxpayer is not required to pay estimated tax for the current year if:

- The taxpayer had no tax liability in the prior year, and
- The taxpayer was a U.S. citizen or resident alien, and
- The current tax year covered a twelve-month period.

The taxpayer also does not have to pay estimated tax if she pays enough through withholding so that the tax due on the return (minus the amounts of tax credits or paid through withholding) is less than $1,000. For a taxpayer with AGI of $150,000 or less, estimated tax payments must be made if she expects the amount owed after withholding and credits to be less than the smaller of:

- 90% of the tax liability on the current year tax return, or
- 100% of the tax liability on the prior-year tax return.

**Note:** For high-income taxpayers with adjusted gross income of *over* $150,000 ($75,000 if married filing separately), the estimated tax safe harbor threshold for the amount owed would be 110% of the previous year's tax liability (rather than 100%).

**77. The answer is A.** Salem is an exempt individual. Teachers temporarily in the United States under a J or Q Visa are considered to be "exempt individuals" for purposes of the substantial presence test. Salem would file Form 1040-NR (not Form 1040). There is a limit to the number of years that a J-1 Visa holder can be exempt from the substantial presence test.

**Note:** The J-1 visa status permits a nonresident alien to temporarily reside in the United States to teach, conduct research, or receive on-the-job training at colleges and universities, hospitals, and research institutions. Generally, a J-1 alien cannot exclude days of presence as a "teacher or trainee" for more than two calendar years. A J-1 alien can exclude U.S. days of presence as a "student" for purposes of the Substantial Presence Test for up to five calendar years.

**78. The answer is D.** In this case, the sales taxes are a *liability*, not income, and are therefore excluded from Regina's gross receipts and deductible expenses, as the taxes are imposed on her buyers and she is merely collecting the taxes on behalf of the state. Note that in certain states, sales taxes are imposed on the seller, and in these states, a seller who collects sales tax from their customers must include the sales taxes in gross receipts and then deducts them when paid (or incurred). Note that when a business pays sales tax in connection with the *purchase* of goods for use in the business, the sales tax is considered a component of the cost of the item purchased. Thus, if the item is depreciable property, the sales tax is added to its depreciable basis. If the item is merchandise for resale or to be used in the production of inventory, the tax is capitalized as a component of inventory. If the sales tax is related to a currently deductible business expense, it is likewise considered part of that expense.

**79. The answer is B.** The wages, interest, alimony, and hobby income are all taxable income and will be reported on Amy's tax return ($26,200 + $5,400 + $7,400 + $5,300 = **$44,300**). Child support, inheritance, and worker's compensation are nontaxable and will not be shown on Amy's tax return. Worker's compensation is not taxable, because it is a form of insurance providing wage replacement and medical benefits to employees injured in the course of employment.

> **Note:** The Tax Cuts and Jobs Act permanently eliminated the deduction for alimony payments for divorces occurring in 2019 or later. However, divorce judgments that were finalized on or before December 31, 2018, are considered "grandfathered" and the old rules apply.

**80. The answer is C.** Based on Vincent's AGI of $45,000, qualifying medical expenses beyond the first $3,375 (or 7.5% of his AGI) would be tax-deductible. Vincent has $8,000 in medical expenses for himself, as well as $2,000 in medical expenses for his daughter. The calculation is as follows:

$$\$45,000 \times 7.5\% \text{ AGI threshold} = \$3,375$$
$$(\$8,000 + \$2,000) = \$10,000 \text{ in qualifying medical expenses}$$
$$\$10,000 - \$3,375 = \mathbf{\$6,625} \text{ allowable deduction}$$

Noncustodial parents who pay medical expenses for a child after a divorce or separation, may deduct those costs on their federal income tax return, even though the other spouse may have custody of the child and/or claim the child. The fact that Vincent does not claim his daughter as a dependent is irrelevant in this case. For the purposes of the medical expense deduction, a child of divorced or separated parents can be treated as a dependent of both parents. This special rule is outlined in IRS Publication 502, *Medical and Dental Expenses*.

**81. The answer is C.** $70,000 will be reported on Zoe's final tax return (Form 1040), and $50,000 will be reported on Form 1041. The question states that the distributive share of partnership income allocable to the <u>entire year</u> was $120,000, which is $10,000 per month ($120,000 ÷ 12 months). Zoe lived until the end of July, so seven months of partnership income would be reported on her final Form 1040 (7 months × $10,000 = $70,000). The remaining income would be reported on the estate income tax return (Form 1041).

**82. The answer is D.** A statutory *nonemployee* is the most likely to be subject to estimated taxes. There are three categories of statutory nonemployees: direct sellers, licensed real estate agents, and certain companion sitters. These taxpayers are treated as self-employed for FICA purposes and are usually required to pay estimated taxes. Answers "A" and "C" are incorrect because household employees and statutory employees would have Medicare and Social Security taxes withheld by their employers. Answer B is wrong because investment income is typically not subject to SE tax.

**83. The answer is C.** Ayden is a U.S. citizen, so he must file using Form 1040. Answer "A" is incorrect because Form 1040-NR is only used by nonresident aliens, not U.S. citizens or U.S. residents. Answer "B" is incorrect because Form 1040-SR is only for seniors who are age 65 or older. Answer "D" is incorrect because Ayden has a filing requirement because his income is over the filing threshold. The fact that he may qualify for the Foreign Earned Income Exclusion is irrelevant; he would have to file a return to claim the exclusion.

**84. The answer is C.** Sybil's gross income includes her wages, interest, and gambling winnings, all of which should be reported on her tax return. Her child support payments are her only nontaxable income. The gambling losses would not be included in the calculation of her gross income. The calculation is figured as follows:

| Type of Income | Amount | Included | Amount |
|---|---|---|---|
| Wages | $80,000 | Yes | $80,000 |
| Interest income | $200 | Yes | $200 |
| Gambling income | $500 | Yes | $500 |
| Child support | $7,000 | No | $0 |
| **Sybil's gross income** | | | **$80,700** |

**85. The answer is D.** Anton must report $16,000 of gambling winnings as taxable income. He should also report the $1,300 withholding on his return. Anton can deduct his gambling losses as an itemized deduction on Schedule A, but the losses are limited to the amount of his gambling winnings. Therefore, Anton cannot deduct more than $16,000 of gambling losses. If a taxpayer does not itemize deductions, he is not allowed to deduct gambling losses. Gambling winnings over certain amounts are reported to a taxpayer on Form W-2G, *Certain Gambling Winnings.*

**Note:** Gambling losses are still deductible against gambling winnings. The TCJA did, however, modify the gambling loss deduction. The TCJA expanded the definition of "gambling losses" to include other expenses incurred in gambling activities, such as travel back and forth from a casino or horse track. Professional gamblers are no longer allowed to generate net operating losses on Schedule C from wagering activities (i.e., their losses are limited to winnings).

**86. The answer is B.** Since Deacon has two qualifying students, he can claim a maximum of **$5,000** ($2,500 × 2) in American Opportunity Credits. Deacon can claim the American Opportunity Credit for Devon and Brianna, but cannot for Keisha, because she is a graduate student who had already completed four years of college as an undergraduate. A taxpayer can claim the American Opportunity Credit for qualified education expenses paid for a dependent child, the taxpayer, or a spouse listed on the return. If a taxpayer has multiple qualifying students, the taxpayer can claim multiple credits on the same return. Deacon may be able to take the Lifetime Learning Credit for Keisha's education expenses if she otherwise qualifies.

**87. The answer is C.** The gift is not taxable, but Tamara and Garfield must report the gift on Form 709. The gift limit in 2023 is $17,000. If both spouses consent to "split" a gift, a married couple can give up to $34,000 in 2023 to a person without making a taxable gift. When a married couple splits a gift, each spouse must generally file his or her own individual gift tax return. However, certain exceptions may apply that allow for only one spouse to file a return if the other spouse signifies consent on the donor spouse's Form 709.

**88. The answer is B.** U.S. Armed Forces members receive many different types of pay and allowances. Some are includible in gross income while others are excludable. U.S. Armed Forces members who have been separated from the military for medical reasons are given *severance pay*, which is generally taxable as wages. If the member receives disability severance pay and is later awarded Veterans Affairs (VA) disability benefits, 100% of the disability severance benefit may be excluded from income. The VA makes the determination that the member is entitled to medical disability benefits, but the determination process can sometimes take several years.

**89. The answer is D.** Edith must file a gift tax return and report the $18,000 gift to Johan. None of the other gifts have a reporting requirement. The general rule is that gifts to a donee that collectively are over $17,000 in 2023 are taxable gifts. However, there are several exceptions to this rule. Generally, the following gifts are not taxable and do not have a reporting requirement:

- Gifts that are not more than the annual exclusion amount (the limit is $17,000 in 2023).
- Tuition or medical expenses paid for someone directly to a school or college[17] or a medical provider (the educational and medical exclusions).
- Gifts to a spouse who is a U.S. citizen (different thresholds apply to spouses who are noncitizens, even if they are legal U.S. residents).
- Contributions to a political organization for its own use.
- Contributions to a church or religious organization (church, synagogue, mosque, etc.).

The donor of a gift is generally responsible for filing the gift tax return and paying gift tax (if any gift tax applies). A gift is not taxable to the recipient but may need to be reported on Form 709, *United States Gift (and Generation-Skipping Transfer) Tax Return.*

---

[17] This exclusion is not limited to just college expenses – any educational organization, such as a private school, also qualifies. Payments directly to the school are not taxable gifts and do not need to be reported (Sect. 2503(e)(2)(A)).

**90. The answer is C.** Hassan must pay an additional 0.9% Medicare tax on his wages over $200,000 ($240,000 - $200,000 = $40,000 over the threshold amount). Hassan's total Additional Medicare Tax is **$360** ($40,000 × 0.9%). Employers are required to withhold the Additional Medicare Tax once an employee's earnings reach $200,000 in a calendar year. Since neither employer is required to withhold the Additional Medicare Tax on Hassan's salary, Hassan must calculate and pay the tax on his individual return. Interest income is not subject to the Additional Medicare Tax, so it is not included in the calculation. Hassan must file Form 8959, *Additional Medicare Tax,* to compute any Additional Medicare Tax due. A taxpayer is liable for the tax if the taxpayer's wages or self-employment income (together with that of his or her spouse if filing a joint return) exceed the threshold amount for the individual's filing status:

| Filing Status | Threshold Amount |
|---|---|
| Married filing jointly | $250,000 |
| Married filing separate | $125,000 |
| Single, HOH, Qualifying Surviving Spouse (QSS) | $200,000 |

**Note:** The *Additional Medicare Tax* was legislated as part of the Affordable Care Act. Under this mandate, in addition to withholding Medicare tax at 1.45%, employers must withhold a 0.9% Additional Medicare Tax from an employee's wages once their earnings reach $200,000 in a calendar year.

**91. The answer is D.** Lottery winnings (and other types of gambling winnings) are typically reported as "other income" on Form 1040. Examples of the types of "other income" include the following:

- Prizes and awards.
- Jury duty pay.
- Alaska Permanent Fund dividends.
- Taxable distributions from a Coverdell education savings account (ESA).
- Hobby income.

**92. The answer is A.** Gunnar has $5,475 of qualifying medical expenses ($4,995 + $405 + $75). The childcare and the hair transplants would not be deductible as a medical expense, but all of the other expenses are specifically allowed in IRS Publication 502. Then he must multiply his AGI of $45,000 by 7.5% to arrive at the deductibility threshold of $3,375. Only medical expenses exceeding $3,375 can be deducted. Therefore, Gunnar has an *allowable* medical expense deduction of **$2,100** (5,475 - 3,375).

**93. The answer is B.** Letty will report **$30,850** of wages on Form 1040. This is the total of her W-2 income and her unreported tip income ($25,600 + $4,950 + $300). The unemployment compensation must be reported as income and the state income tax refund may have to be reported if Letty had itemized her deductions in the prior year and received a tax benefit from the state tax deduction, but neither would be reported on the return as wages.

**94. The answer is D.** Foster can claim an AOTC credit of 100% of the $2,000 in qualifying expenses. The maximum amount of the AOTC is $2,500 per student, per year. The credit is calculated as follows: 100% of the first $2,000 of qualified education expenses and 25% of the *next* $2,000 of qualified education expenses paid for each eligible student.

**95. The answer is B.** Nathaniel's deductions from his gross estate are first figured as follows:

| | |
|---|---|
| Funeral and burial costs | $23,000 |
| Attorney's fees | $37,950 |
| Debts owed at the time of death | $86,500 |
| Unpaid mortgage on the decedent's primary residence | $723,700 |
| Property taxes accrued <u>after</u> death | Not Allowable |
| **Amount deductible from Nathaniel's Gross Estate** | **$871,150** |

Certain deductions are available to reduce the Estate Tax. These amounts would be deductible from the "gross estate" in order to figure the "taxable estate" on Form 706. The most common of these is the *Marital Deduction.* All property that is included in the gross estate and passes to the surviving spouse is eligible for the marital deduction if the surviving spouse is a U.S. citizen. The property must pass "outright." Examples of other estate tax deductions include:

- Charitable Deduction: If the decedent leaves property to a qualifying charity, it is deductible from the gross estate.
- Mortgages, property taxes, and debts owed by the decedent <u>at the time of death</u>.
- Administration expenses of the estate (such as lawyer's fees and accounting costs).
- Funeral and burial expenses.
- Losses during estate administration.

These deductions are allowable *in addition* to the estate and gift tax exemption. For 2023, the estate and gift tax exemption is $12,920,000 per taxpayer. So, using the figures above, the amount of Nathaniel's *taxable estate* would be figured as follows:

| | |
|---|---|
| Gross estate on the date of death | $18,000,000 |
| Amount deductible from the Gross Estate | ($871,150) |
| Estate Tax Exemption in 2023 | ($12,920,000) |
| **Nathaniel's Taxable Estate** | **$4,208,850** |

Since the property taxes in the question accrued *after* the date of Nathaniel's death, they would not be includable in the calculation of the taxable estate. Since the property would pass to a daughter (instead of a surviving spouse), then Nathaniel's estate would be subject to the estate tax.

**96. The answer is D.** An annulled marriage is considered void from its inception. Theodore is deemed to be single, and he must also file amended returns (Form 1040-X) claiming "**single**" for all tax years that are affected by the annulment and not closed by the statute of limitations.

**97. The answer is B.** Jaxson has $1,100 of net long-term capital gains ($1,600 gain - $500 loss). The gain on the Hibbert, Inc. stock is short-term because the shares were not held for more than a year.

| Activity | Bought | Sold | Gain/Loss | Character |
|---|---|---|---|---|
| 1,400 shares at $3,000 (basis: $1,400) | 1/3/2020 | 12/1/2023 | $1,600 | LT gain |
| 200 shares at $500 (basis: $1,000) | 1/3/2017 | 12/25/2023 | ($500) | LT loss |
| 50 shares at $1,700 (basis: $1,500) | 2/1/2023 | 9/12/2023 | $200 | ST gain |

**98. The answer is D.** Naomi may be eligible for the Retirement Savings Contributions Credit. None of the other credits listed would be applicable. Naomi would not qualify for the Child and Dependent Care Credit, or the Credit for Other Dependents, because she does not have any dependents. Her taxable income is also above the threshold for the Earned Income Tax Credit (for taxpayers with no dependents). The Retirement Savings Contributions Credit is between 10% – 50% of eligible contributions to IRAs and retirement plans up to a maximum credit of $1,000 ($2,000 MFJ). The 2023 income limitations are as follows:

| Credit % | MFJ | HOH | Single, QSS, MFS |
|---|---|---|---|
| 50% | AGI not more than $43,500 | AGI not more than $32,625 | AGI not more than $21,750 |
| 20% | $43,501- $47,500 | $32,626 - $35,625 | $21,751 - $23,750 |
| 10% | $47,501 - $73,000 | $35,626 - $54,750 | $23,751 - $36,500 |
| No Credit | more than $73,000 | more than $54,750 | more than $36,500 |

**99. The answer is D.** Kendra can use **$22,000** of passive income from the partnership investment to offset her **$24,000** rental loss. The remaining rental losses of **$2,000** ($22,000 - $24,000) would need to be carried over to the following year. Even though she materially participated in the rental activity, she must carry over her excess rental losses because her modified adjusted gross income is over the phaseout threshold of $100,000. An individual may deduct up to $25,000 of real estate loss per year as long as their adjusted gross income is under the phaseout threshold. This is also called the special "$25,000 rental loss allowance." However, if the taxpayer's MAGI is $150,000 or more ($75,000 or more if married filing separately), then no deduction can be claimed for a rental activity loss for the year. Since Kendra's wages exceed $150,000, she must carryover any of her excess losses to the following year.

**100. The answer is C.** Maeve and Slade are both eligible to claim a 50% credit for their IRA contributions; therefore, Maeve's credit is $500 ($1,000 contribution × 50%), and Slade's credit is worth $900 ($1,800 contribution × 50%). So, on a joint return, they are allowed a **$1,400 credit** ($500 for Maeve and $900 for Slade). The credit limits and AGI thresholds for 2023 are as follows:

| Credit % | MFJ | HOH | Single, QSS, MFS |
|---|---|---|---|
| 50% | AGI not more than $43,500 | AGI not more than $32,625 | AGI not more than $21,750 |
| 20% | $43,501- $47,500 | $32,626 - $35,625 | $21,751 - $23,750 |
| 10% | $47,501 - $73,000 | $35,626 - $54,750 | $23,751 - $36,500 |
| No Credit | more than $73,000 | more than $54,750 | more than $36,500 |

**Note:** This credit is also called the "Saver's Credit." The IRS uses the two names interchangeably on the IRS website as well as in IRS publications.

# #2 Sample Exam: Individuals

**(Please test yourself first, then check the correct answers at the end of this exam.)**

1. Heath is 61 and covered by a retirement plan at work. In 2023, he received a Form 1099-R showing a $3,000 amount in box 1. In addition, the "IRA/SEP/SIMPLE" box is checked (box 7). What does this indicate?

A. Heath has made an IRA-type distribution.
B. Heath has received an annuity.
C. Heath has made a prohibited transaction.
D. Heath has made an excess contribution to his retirement plan.

2. Income in respect of a decedent (IRD):

A. Is taxed on the final return of the deceased taxpayer.
B. Is never included in the decedent's estate.
C. Is taxable income that was received by the decedent before death.
D. May be subject to estate tax.

3. Everly has a Health Savings Account (HSA) through her employer. Which of the following would _not_ be a qualifying medical expense for HSA purposes in 2023?

A. Dental services.
B. Menstrual care products.
C. Health club dues.
D. Over-the-counter medications.

4. Victoria and Colton divorced in 2017. Under their divorce settlement, Victoria must pay her ex-husband $15,000 in alimony per year, which she pays in equal installments each month. She is also required to pay his ongoing medical expenses for a heart condition he acquired during their marriage. In 2023, Colton's medical expenses were $11,400. She paid $10,000 of the medical expenses directly to the hospital. The other $1,400 she gave directly to Colton after getting a copy of the doctor's bill. How much of these payments can be properly deducted by Victoria as alimony?

A. $15,000
B. $16,400
C. $25,000
D. $26,400

5. Prescott is 55 years old and single. He owns two rental properties and works part-time as a cashier in a grocery store. He is not a real estate professional and reports his rental income on Schedule E. He has the following income for the year:

| | |
|---|---:|
| W-2 wages from his part-time job | $5,200 |
| Interest income | $122 |
| Capital gain from the sale of stock | $5,900 |
| Rental income from property #1 | $12,000 |
| Rental income from property #2 | $30,000 |
| Dividend income | $530 |
| State income tax refund from a prior year | $2,300 |

Prescott wants to fund his traditional IRA this year. What is the *maximum* that he can contribute for the 2023 tax year?

A. $5,200
B. $6,000
C. $6,500
D. $7,500

6. Sloane owns a business office building. She allows her church to use the building rent-free for six months. Sloane normally rents the office for $600 a month. Similar offices are renting for $700 a month in the same building. How much can Sloane deduct as a charitable deduction on her Schedule A?

A. $0
B. $3,600
C. $4,200
D. $7,200

7. Wilson rents a two-bedroom apartment from his landlord. He does not own the apartment. Wilson is a self-employed bookkeeper and works exclusively out of a home office. In 2023, Wilson paid $1,000 a month in rent for his apartment. He also spent $50 a month in utilities. His home office is 240 square feet. The total square footage of his apartment is 1,200 square feet. He decides to deduct "actual expenses" for his home office. Ignoring any income limitations, what is Wilson's maximum allowable deduction for home office expenses?

A. $0
B. $1,200
C. $2,520
D. $12,600

8. Clarence incurs the following medical expenses in 2023.

- Lasik vision correction surgery: $2,300
- Prescription medications: $1,200
- Laboratory fees for bloodwork: $1,100
- Medical marijuana (he has a prescription): $800
- Health club dues: $724
- Prescription eyeglasses: $500

Clarence's AGI is $40,000. How much of his qualifying medical expenses are deductible on Schedule A, *after* the application of the AGI limit?

A. $375
B. $435
C. $2,100
D. $5,100

9. Sebastian is unmarried and 29 years old. He is permanently and totally disabled. He lived with his mother, Olivia, all year. Olivia is unmarried, age 58, and earned $32,000 in wages during the year. Olivia pays all the rent and utilities for the apartment that they both reside in. Sebastian earned $7,100 in wages at a part-time workshop for disabled individuals. Sebastian does not provide more than one-half of his own support. Based on this information, can Olivia claim Sebastian as a qualifying child for Head of Household and EITC purposes?

A. Sebastian is a qualifying child for EITC purposes but not for Head of Household.
B. Sebastian is a qualifying child for Head of Household but not for EITC purposes.
C. Sebastian is not a qualifying child for Head of Household or for EITC purposes.
D. Sebastian is a qualifying child for Head of Household and EITC purposes.

10. Laureen works full-time as a payroll supervisor for a regional bank. During the year, she was selected for jury duty. Her employer has a policy which compensates employees for the time spent in jury service. She will receive her full salary while she serves on the jury, but she is required to remit the fees received for her jury service back to her employer. She serves 25 days on the jury and receives $15.00 per day, so a total of $375. Since she is required to remit the jury duty fees to her employer, how should this be reported?

A. Laureen can deduct any remitted jury duty pay as an adjustment to income.
B. Laureen can deduct any remitted jury duty pay as an itemized deduction.
C. Laureen cannot deduct the remitted jury duty pay.
D. Laureen can offset her wage income by the amount that she was forced to remit to her employer.

11. Elijah is unmarried and files as single. In 2023, he worked for two different employers. Elijah received two Forms W-2: one showing wages of $5,000 and another showing wage income of $18,500. He also had $4,000 in long-term capital losses from a stock sale, and a $130 early withdrawal penalty from a certificate of deposit. He had no other items of gain or loss during the year. What is his adjusted gross income (AGI) on Form 1040?

A. $19,500
B. $20,370
C. $20,500
D. $21,500

12. Julie's husband, Austin, died on June 3, 2023. The value of Austin's gross estate was $5 million on the date of his death, so an estate tax return does not need to be filed. However, Julie decides to file an estate tax return anyway. What is the purpose of filing an estate tax return (Form 706) in this situation?

A. To claim the unlimited marital deduction.
B. To calculate the estate tax owed in advance.
C. To properly distribute assets to all his heirs.
D. To elect portability of the DSUE amount.

13. Which of the following situations would qualify an individual taxpayer for an automatic tax filing extension?

A. Having a sick pet.
B. Living in a federally declared disaster area.
C. Traveling abroad for temporary work.
D. Owning a business that has incurred losses.

14. Blakely owns a vacation condo near the Park City Mountain Resort in Utah. She visits the ski home most weekends and spends the entire months of December and January there. When she is not at the ski condo, she lives in an apartment that she rents in Salt Lake City, Utah. She does not own the apartment in Salt Lake City. She works primarily online from her computer. She is considering selling the condo this year. What is Blakely's primary residence for purposes of the Section 121 exclusion?

A. Her ski condo in Park City.
B. She is considered a transient for tax purposes.
C. She has the right to choose which home would be classified as her primary residence.
D. Her apartment in Salt Lake City.

15. Arthur is divorced and has sole legal custody of his two children, Andrew, age 8, and Cassandra, age 5. Arthur files as head of household. He earned $150,000 in wages in 2023. He has no other income. Arthur meets all the requirements to claim the Child Tax Credit for his two children. What is the maximum Child Tax Credit that Arthur is eligible for in 2023?

A. $0
B. $2,000
C. $4,000
D. $6,000

16. For the purposes of determining the residency for a qualifying child, who is deemed the custodial parent?

A. The parent with whom the child lived for the greater number of nights during the year.
B. The parent who has legal custody under a divorce or separation agreement.
C. The parent who decides to claim the child first.
D. The parent who financially supports the child.

17. Skylar is single and earned $48,000 in 2023 working as a nature photographer. She is a U.S. citizen and a legal resident of Brazil. She spends about 5 months in Brazil every year taking nature photographs of the Amazon rainforest. The remaining time she lives in Florida, where she maintains an apartment. As of December 31, 2023, she had the following funds held in foreign bank accounts in three separate Brazilian banks:

- Bank Account #1: $8,000
- Bank Account #2: $9,000
- Bank Account #3: $35,000

All the amounts listed are shown in the value of U.S. dollars. She also had an additional $16,000 in a U.S. checking account. What is Skylar's federal tax filing requirement for these funds?

A. None. Funds held in offshore accounts are not reportable to the U.S. government.
B. She must file an FBAR.
C. She must file Form 8938.
D. She must file both an FBAR and Form 8938.

18. Wesley has a part-time nanny who works in his home. Wesley paid his nanny $2,450 in wages during 2023. Which of the following statements is correct?

A. Wesley does not have to report Social Security and Medicare taxes on the nanny's wages.
B. The nanny's income is not taxable because it is under the reporting threshold for household employees.
C. No reporting is required by either party if the wages are paid in cash.
D. Wesley can deduct the nanny's wages on Schedule C since she is his employee.

19. Carter and Melissa are married and file jointly. They are in the process of adopting a foreign child from Russia. Carter and Melissa paid qualified adoption expenses of $3,000 in 2021, $4,000 in 2022, and $5,000 in 2023. The adoption became final on March 6, 2023. How should Carter and Melissa treat these adoption expenses on their tax return?

A. They can claim an adoption credit of $3,000 in 2021, $4,000 in 2022, and $5,000 in 2023.
B. They may claim $12,000 in qualified adoption expenses as an adoption credit in 2023.
C. They may claim $7,000 in qualified adoption expenses in 2022 and $5,000 in 2023.
D. Foreign adoptions are not eligible for the adoption credit.

20. Laurent dies on March 18, 2023. He had approximately $18 million in assets at the time of his death, so an estate tax return must be filed. The executor of Laurent's estate chooses to elect the alternate valuation date for the estate. What is the alternate valuation date of Laurent's estate?

A. May 15, 2023.
B. September 18, 2023.
C. December 31, 2023.
D. March 18, 2024.

21. On April 20, 2023, Willow received a parcel of land as a gift from her uncle, Hudson. The fair market value (FMV) of the property on the date of the gift was $13,800. Hudson's original cost basis in the land was $8,700. He owned the land for more than ten years before he gifted it to his niece. After the deed was transferred, Willow decided to demolish an existing concrete foundation on the property. The cost of the demolition was $3,200. There were no more improvements done to the property during the year. Based on this information, what is Willow's basis in the land at the end of the year?

A. $8,700
B. $10,600
C. $11,900
D. $13,800

22. Josiah is 34 and wants to contribute to a traditional IRA for 2023. He requests an extension to file his tax return, but ends up filing his tax return early, on February 28, 2024, taking a $6,500 deduction for an IRA contribution. What is the *latest* date that Josiah can contribute to his traditional IRA?

A. February 28, 2024
B. April 15, 2024
C. June 15, 2024
D. October 15, 2024

23. What is the difference between "U.S.-source income" and "foreign source" income?

A. There is no difference between the two for a U.S. citizen that has a filing requirement.
B. Foreign source income comes from a foreign country, while U.S.-source income comes from the U.S.
C. Foreign source income originates only from foreign entities.
D. U.S.-source income is determined by tax treaties; foreign source income is only determined by internal tax laws of various countries.

24. Caroline and Xavier are married and file jointly. They had the following income in 2023:

| Xavier | Amount | Caroline | Amount |
|--------|--------|----------|--------|
| Wages | $155,000 | Wages | $176,000 |
| Commissions | $18,000 | Court settlement | $56,000 |

Neither of their employers withheld the Additional Medicare Tax from their wages. Caroline's court settlement was from an auto accident where she suffered a broken leg. What amount, if any, do Caroline and Xavier owe for the *Additional Medicare Tax* in 2023 (the threshold is $250,000 for couples filing jointly)?

A. $0
B. $729
C. $891
D. $3,141

25. Marley is 62 and unmarried. He works full-time as a computer engineer. He owns one residential rental property. He is not a real estate professional. In 2023, he had the following income:

| W-2 Wages | $210,000 |
|-----------|----------|
| Traditional IRA distributions | $25,000 |
| Capital gains from the sale of stock | $12,000 |
| Rental income reported on Schedule E | $15,000 |
| Ordinary dividends | $9,000 |
| **Total MAGI** | **$271,000** |

What amount does Marley owe for the Net Investment Income Tax (the threshold for single filers is $200,000)?

A. $0
B. $1,368
C. $2,318
D. $2,698

26. Leilani has lived apart from her husband for several years. Leilani and her husband are not legally separated and neither spouse has filed for divorce. She does not have any children or other dependents. She files separately from her husband. In 2023, Leilani earned $49,000 in wages (which is her only income for the year). She also incurs $25,400 of passive losses from a rental duplex in which she actively participated. She owns the rental property outright (it is not jointly owned with her husband). She is not a real estate professional, but she actively participated in the rental activity by choosing her own tenants and collecting the rent herself. How much of her rental losses are allowable on Schedule E on her MFS return?

A. $0
B. $12,500
C. $25,000
D. $25,400

27. Lennox is 35, married, and has a traditional IRA through his credit union. Rollover rules allow Lennox to do which one of the following without incurring any income tax or penalty?

A. Rollover funds from his traditional IRA plan to a Roth IRA account.
B. Rollover his traditional IRA into his spouse's traditional IRA.
C. Rollover into a 529 educational savings plan.
D. Rollover funds into a 401(k) plan.

28. Madeline paid $280 for six tickets to a fundraising dinner at her church. The value of the dinner (printed on the ticket) was $20 per person, and her family attended the dinner and enjoyed the meal. All the proceeds from the dinner will go to the church. Madeline itemizes her deductions. How much can Madeline potentially deduct as a charitable donation on her Schedule A?

A. $0
B. $120
C. $160
D. $280

29. In 2023, Landon obtained a home equity loan totaling $100,000. He used the proceeds of the loan to build an additional bedroom on his property. The fair market value of his home is $430,000, and he carries an additional $130,000 mortgage that was used to purchase the home. Which of the following statements is correct?

A. Landon can deduct the interest from the mortgage and home equity loan on Schedule A.
B. Landon can deduct the mortgage interest on Schedule A, but not the home equity loan.
C. Landon can deduct the interest from the home equity loan on Schedule A, but not the mortgage.
D. Landon cannot deduct any of the interest on Schedule A.

30. Joshua is unmarried and 47 years old. He has a dependent son who is 15 years old. Joshua qualifies for head of household filing status. In 2023, Joshua's wage income was $23,000, and he also had investment income from the sale of stock. What is the maximum amount of investment income that Joshua can have before he is disqualified from claiming the Earned Income Tax Credit (EITC) in 2023?

A. $2,600
B. $3,650
C. $4,600
D. $11,000

31. Robin is age 25 and a full-time college student. She is the beneficiary of a Section 529 Education Savings Account that was set up by her grandparents years ago. Robin withdraws $10,000 from the 529 account in 2023. She wants to use the funds to pay for as many qualifying expenses as possible, without having to pay any tax on the distributions. Which of the following expenses would not be a qualifying expense for use of the distributed funds?

A. On-campus housing.
B. Books and supplies.
C. Transportation and travel costs to her college.
D. Paying down $10,000 of her student loans.

32. Talia is single and 51 years old and covered by a 401(k) retirement plan at work. Her salary was $73,000 in 2023. She also had $14,000 in interest income, making her modified AGI $87,000. Talia also made a $7,500 traditional IRA contribution for 2023. How should this contribution be treated on Talia's tax return?

A. Talia cannot deduct her IRA contribution. She must designate this contribution as a nondeductible contribution.
B. Since Talia is already covered by a workplace retirement plan, she cannot make a contribution to a traditional IRA. She must withdraw the contribution or incur a penalty.
C. Talia can fully deduct her traditional IRA contribution on Form 1040 as an adjustment to income.
D. This is a prohibited transaction. Talia's IRA is disqualified, and she will pay a 10% penalty.

33. Weston turned 72 on July 30, 2023. He is still employed full-time and has a Roth IRA. When must he start taking required minimum distributions from his Roth IRA account?

A. December 31, 2023.
B. April 1, 2024.
C. April 15, 2024.
D. Never.

34. Trinity and Wesson file jointly and claim their two children as dependents. They plan to itemize their deductions on Schedule A. Last year, the family accumulated the following in unreimbursed medical expenses:

- Vitamins for general health: $120
- Prescription medications imported from Canada: $240
- Hearing aids for Wesson, who is partially deaf: $320
- Prescription eyeglasses for the entire family: $1,000
- Chiropractor fees, not covered by insurance: $4,400
- Acupuncture for Trinity: $1,250

Ignoring any income limitations, what is the amount of their *qualifying* medical expenses?

A. $5,720
B. $5,960
C. $6,970
D. $7,220


35. On the one-year anniversary at her new job, Faith's employer gave her restricted stock in the company with the condition that it would be forfeited if she did not complete three years of service with the company. The stock's FMV is $30,000. How much should she include in her income for the current year, and what would be her basis in the stock?

A. Income of $30,000; no basis.
B. No income; basis of $30,000.
C. Income of $30,000; basis of $30,000.
D. No income; no basis.

36. Ezra and his wife, Dawn, both attend graduate school. They file jointly, and their combined AGI is $61,000. In 2023, they had the following expenses paid to their university for graduate tuition and required books:

- Ezra: $4,800
- Dawn: $6,900

They had both previously completed four years of postsecondary education prior to attending graduate school, and both have bachelor's degrees. Based on the information given, what is the maximum amount of education credits they may claim on their joint return?

A. Ezra is eligible for a $960 Lifetime Learning Credit, and Dawn is eligible for a $1,380 Lifetime Learning Credit.
B. Ezra and Dawn are each eligible for a $2,500 American Opportunity Credit.
C. Ezra and Dawn are eligible for a maximum $2,000 Lifetime Learning Credit.
D. Ezra and Dawn are eligible for a $4,000 Lifetime Learning Credit.

37. Paloma is married, but she files separately from her spouse. In 2023, Paloma plans to itemize her deductions. Her husband also plans to itemize. Her state and local income taxes totaled $12,580 for the year. What is Paloma's maximum deduction for State and Local Taxes on Schedule A in 2023?

A. $0
B. $5,000
C. $10,000
D. $12,580.

38. Bryan and Tasha are married and have always filed jointly. On January 12, 2023, Bryan dies. Bryan's final will names Nolan, his family law attorney, as the executor of his estate. Bryan's widow, Tasha, meets someone new and remarries on December 20, 2023. Tasha plans to file jointly with her new husband. Which filing status should the executor use for Bryan's final tax return?

A. Married Filing Separately.
B. Qualifying Surviving Spouse (QSS).
C. Married Filing Jointly or Married Filing Separately.
D. Single.

39. On January 3, 2023, Greg, age 42, quits his job. He decides to roll his 401(k) into a traditional IRA. He meant for this to be a trustee-to-trustee rollover, but he made an error when filling out the forms, and the funds were sent to him directly in the form of a check. What must he do in order to avoid paying income tax and an early withdrawal penalty on the distribution?

A. Greg must pay income tax and a 10% penalty on the entire distribution.
B. The distribution is subject to a 6% mandatory excise tax which he must pay.
C. Greg has until April 15, 2023, to deposit an amount equal to the total gross distribution into an IRA.
D. Greg has 60 days to deposit an amount equal to the gross distribution into an IRA.

40. Which of the following taxpayers cannot claim the Earned Income Tax Credit in 2023?

A. Esme, age 42, with a valid Social Security number and an 8-year-old foster child who is her dependent.
B. Diallo, age 33, who files jointly with Hadiza, who is a nonresident alien. Diallo has a valid Social Security Number and Hadiza has an ITIN. They claim one dependent child who is 6 years old and has a valid SSN.
C. Anastasia, age 62, with a valid Social Security number, but no dependents.
D. Contessa, age 52, who has earned income from a foreign country.

41. Axel donated to his church several times during the year. All of his donations went to the same church. Which of the following charitable gifts does not meet IRS substantiation (recordkeeping) requirements?

A. A $210 donation paid by a check. Axel has a copy of the canceled check, but no receipt from the church.
B. A $340 donation made in cash. Axel has a contemporaneous receipt from the church.
C. A contribution of noncash property worth $5,200 (a painting). Axel has a written receipt from the church, but no appraisal.
D. Charitable mileage totaling $150 that was incurred while Axel was volunteering. Axel does not have a receipt, but he has a written mileage log.

42. Nikos, a full-time graduate student with no compensation, marries Heather during the year. Both are age 31. Heather earns taxable wages of $79,000. Heather wants to contribute the maximum to her traditional IRA. If Nikos and Heather file jointly, how much can each contribute to a traditional IRA in 2023?

A. Heather and Nikos can each contribute $6,500 to their respective traditional IRAs.
B. Heather can contribute $6,500 to her traditional IRA. Nikos cannot contribute to an IRA because he does not have any qualifying compensation.
C. Heather and Nikos can each contribute $7,500 to their respective traditional IRAs.
D. Heather can contribute $7,500 to her traditional IRA. Nikos cannot make an IRA contribution.

43. Reuben purchases a new car for $24,000 cash on December 2, 2023. This is his personal vehicle and will not be used for business. On January 30, 2024, Reuben receives a $2,000 rebate check from the manufacturer of the vehicle. How should this be reported on his tax return (choose the best answer)?

A. The rebate is not taxable and does not have to be reported.
B. The rebate is taxable and must be reported on Reuben's 2023 tax return.
C. The rebate is not taxable, but Reuben must reduce his basis in the car by $2,000.
D. The rebate is taxable and must be reported on Reuben's 2024 tax return.

44. Which of the following is NOT a test to determine whether or not a dependent is a "qualifying child" of a taxpayer?

A. Relationship test.
B. Gross income test.
C. Residency test.
D. Support test.

45. Victor owns several investments. He has the following transactions in 2023:

- $1,000 capital loss on Abbot Inc. stock he purchased on January 15, 2023, and sold on November 30, 2023.
- He inherited an undeveloped parcel of land on February 12, 2023. He sold the empty lot for a $5,200 gain on April 14, 2023.
- $2,000 gain on the sale of Acutrim Inc. stock he purchased on March 15, 2019, and sold on June 15, 2023.

What is the amount and nature of each of Victor's gains and losses?

A. Victor has a net $2,000 short-term capital loss and a $5,200 long-term capital gain.
B. Victor has a net $7,200 long-term capital gain. The long-term capital loss is not deductible.
C. Victor has a net $1,000 short-term capital loss and a $5,200 long-term capital gain.
D. Victor has a $1,000 short-term capital loss and a $7,200 long-term capital gain.

46. Audrey, who files single, paid the following taxes and fees during the tax year:

| State income tax | $2,000 |
| Real estate taxes on her primary residence in Maine | $1,900 |
| Real estate taxes on a vacation home in Colorado | $2,400 |
| Real estate taxes on a vacation condo in Cancun, Mexico | $1,400 |
| Personal property tax on DMV auto license | $100 |
| Homeowners' association fees on her primary residence | $250 |

Audrey plans to itemize her deductions. What is her total allowable deduction for taxes on Schedule A?

A. $1,900
B. $4,000
C. $6,400
D. $7,800

47. Tyson is 21 years old and lives with his parents, who provide the majority of his support. He makes $4,900 in wages from a part-time job in 2023. Tyson enrolled in a college degree program in January. He attended college full-time for three months (January, February, and March) and then drops out of the program before finishing the semester. Can Tyson's parents claim him as a dependent?

A. Tyson's parents can claim him as a qualifying relative.
B. Tyson's parents can claim him as a qualifying child.
C. Tyson's parents cannot claim him as a dependent.
D. Tyson's parents can claim him as a foster child.

48. Felicity, age twelve, has a small role in a popular television series. She made $65,000 as a child actress during the tax year, but her parents put all the money in a trust fund to pay for her college. Her parents have a joint AGI of $61,000. Felicity lived at home with her parents all year. Does Felicity meet the tests in order for her parents to claim her as a dependent?

A. Felicity meets the support test, and her parents can claim her as a dependent.
B. Felicity does not meet the support test, and her parents cannot legally claim her as a dependent.
C. Since Felicity made the most money in the household, she can legally file her own tax return as single and claim her parents as dependents.
D. Felicity should file her own tax return. Her parents should not claim her as a dependent.

49. Jayden has a healthcare FSA (flexible spending arrangement) through his employer. Jayden's employer contributed $2,500 to his FSA. Jayden also contributes an additional $200 to the FSA from his own personal funds. Which of the following statements is correct?

A. The amounts that Jayden contributed to his FSA must be reported on his individual return and are subject to an ACA tax.
B. The amounts contributed to Jayden's FSA are not subject to federal income taxes, but the full amount is subject to Social Security tax and Medicare tax.
C. The amounts contributed to Jayden's FSA are not subject to employment or federal income taxes. Both the employer and employee may contribute.
D. Jayden cannot contribute to an FSA. The FSA must be fully funded by the employer via salary reduction in order for the contributions to be exempt from tax.

50. Wade, a U.S. citizen, is married to Marianna, a Greek citizen. Their son, Linus, was born in Greece during the tax year. Does their child meet the tests in order for Wade to claim his newborn son as a qualifying child?

A. Wade's son is a qualifying child. Linus is a U.S. citizen because his father is a U.S. citizen.
B. Wade's son is not a qualifying child because the child was born overseas.
C. Wade's son is a qualifying relative, not a qualifying child.
D. Wade's son is not a qualifying child because the child does not pass the physical presence test.

51. Which of the following deductions is not permitted as an *adjustment to income* on Form 1040?

A. Self-employed health insurance.
B. Property taxes paid on a personal residence.
C. Alimony paid pursuant to a post-2018 agreement.
D. Penalty on the early withdrawal of a certificate of deposit.

52. On February 10, 2023, Serenity purchased a plot of undeveloped land in Hawaii, intending to build a home. The lot cost $239,000. The following month, Serenity spent another $12,000 clearing and grading the land to get it ready for construction. Before construction could begin, Serenity was approached by a developer who wished to purchase the land. Serenity agrees to the sale, and the property is sold on December 29, 2023, for $329,000. What is the nature and amount of Serenity's gain on the sale?

A. $0 gain.
B. $78,000 short-term capital gain.
C. $90,000 long-term capital gain.
D. $102,000 short-term capital gain.

53. Which of the following would never be considered a taxable recovery?

A. Insurance reimbursement.
B. State income tax refund.
C. Rebate of a deduction itemized the prior year on Schedule A.
D. Federal income tax refund.

54. Kenzie is a beneficiary of her deceased uncle's estate. In 2023, she receives a $1,500 distribution of nonpassive income from the estate. How will this distribution be reported to Kenzie, and how should she report the income on her own individual tax return?

A. The distribution from the estate would be reported to Kenzie on Schedule K-1 (Form 1041). The amounts would be reported on her Schedule E (Form 1040).
B. The distribution from the estate would be reported to Kenzie on Schedule K-1 (Form 1041). The amounts would be reported as other income on Schedule 1.
C. The distribution from the estate would be reported to Kenzie on Schedule K-1 (Form 1041). The amounts would be reported on Schedule D (Form 1040).
D. A distribution from an estate is never taxable to the beneficiary, only to the estate.

55. Fletcher and Samantha sold their home on May 7, 2023. Through April 30, 2023 (before the sale), they made home mortgage interest payments of $12,200. The settlement statement (HUD-1) for the sale of the home showed an additional $50 of interest for the six-day period in May up to, but not including, the date of sale. They also incurred a mortgage prepayment penalty of $2,000. In May, they paid $120 in late payment fees to their mortgage lender due to a missed payment. How much is their allowable mortgage interest deduction?

A. $12,200
B. $12,250
C. $12,370
D. $14,370

56. Yousef is married, but files separately from his wife (MFS). In 2023, Yousef had $185,000 in self-employment income from his sole proprietorship. He also received $15,000 in taxable income from a residential rental that he solely owns. He is not a real estate professional. How much Additional Medicare Tax will Yousef owe in 2023 (the threshold for MFS is $125,000)?

A. $540
B. $675
C. $940
D. $1,251

57. Priscilla owns a vacation home in Miami, Florida. In 2023, she rented the home online for two weeks (14 days), earning $1,200. She also lived in the home for four months. Priscilla paid $5,000 in mortgage interest on the home. For the remainder of the year, the home was vacant. What is the proper treatment of this activity?

A. Priscilla does not have to report the rental income. The mortgage interest is deductible on Schedule A as an itemized deduction.
B. The rental income should be reported on Schedule E, and the mortgage interest is deductible on Schedule A as an itemized deduction.
C. The rental income and mortgage interest should be reported on Schedule E.
D. The rental income should be reported as other income on Form 1040. The mortgage interest is not deductible since it is a vacation home.

58. Three years ago, Lenny bought 500 shares of Belker Systems, Inc. stock for $1,500, including his broker's commission. On April 6, 2023, Belker Systems distributed a 2% nontaxable stock dividend (10 shares). Three months later, on July 6, 2023, Lenny sold all 510 shares of his stock in Belker Systems for $2,030. What is the nature and the amount of Lenny's gain?

A. $510 Long-term capital gain.
B. $530 short-term capital gain.
C. $530 long-term capital gain.
D. $510 short-term capital gain.

59. Which of the following deductions is an adjustment to income in 2023, rather than an itemized deduction?

A. Federal estate tax on income in respect of a decedent.
B. Student loan interest deduction.
C. Gambling losses.
D. Real estate taxes paid.

60. Antoinette is the sole proprietor of a small craft store that had a net profit of $25,000 in 2023. Her husband, Marty, is also self-employed. Marty runs a carpentry business that had a net loss of $1,500. Antoinette and Marty file jointly. How should this income and loss be reported?

A. They may file a single Schedule C netting the income and loss from both businesses. The Schedule SE will show total earnings subject to SE tax of $23,500.

B. Antoinette must file a Schedule C showing her net profit of $25,000, and Marty must file his own Schedule C for the carpentry business showing his net loss of $1,500. Their Schedule SE will show total earnings subject to SE tax of $23,500.

C. Antoinette must file a Schedule C showing her net profit of $25,000, and Marty must file his own Schedule C for the carpentry business showing his net loss of $1,500. Antoinette's Schedule SE will show total earnings subject to SE tax of $25,000. Marty's Schedule SE will show a credit for $1,500 (the amount of his loss).

D. Antoinette must file a Schedule C showing her net profit of $25,000, and Marty must file his own Schedule C for the carpentry business showing his net loss of $1,500. Antoinette's Schedule SE will show total earnings subject to SE tax of $25,000.

61. Porter, age 67, and Norah, age 59, are married and file jointly. Porter and Norah are both U.S. citizens. Porter is retired and draws Social Security. He is covered by Medicare. Norah works part-time at a local bakery. Their combined AGI is $30,500 in 2023. Norah's employer does not offer health insurance. Norah wants health insurance, but she is too young to enroll in Medicare. Can Norah qualify for the Premium Tax Credit if she obtains health coverage through the Marketplace?

A. No. Porter is on Medicare, so if they file jointly, his coverage will disqualify her from eligibility.

B. Norah may be eligible for a PTC if she enrolls in Marketplace coverage.

C. Norah must file a separate return from her husband in order to qualify for the PTC.

D. Since Porter and Norah are married and file jointly, they must both enroll in Marketplace coverage in order to qualify for the Premium Tax Credit.

62. Tucker was laid off from his job on March 30, 2023, when his employer relocated to a different state. Tucker earned $16,000 in wages until he was laid off. He also received worker's compensation benefits from a work-related injury that he sustained in January 2023, approximately two months before he was laid off. His worker's compensation benefits totaled $14,600 for the year. Tucker got lucky in December and won $20,000 on a lottery ticket. How much should Tucker report as gross income in 2023?

A. $16,000
B. $30,600
C. $36,000
D. $55,600

63. In the prior year, Easton paid $1,700 for medical expenses. Easton itemizes his deductions, and after figuring out his allowable deductions, he claimed a $200 medical deduction on his prior-year Schedule A. On February 5, 2023, Easton received an unexpected $500 reimbursement from his medical insurance company for his prior-year expenses. How should this reimbursement be reported by Easton in 2023?

A. Easton should amend his prior-year return and adjust his medical deduction amounts.
B. Easton must include $200 in his 2023 taxable income.
C. Easton must include $500 in his 2023 taxable income.
D. The recovery is not taxable and does not have to be reported.

64. Edwina's main home in Florida was destroyed by a hurricane in 2023. The county where the home was located was later declared a federal disaster area. Edwina's basis in the home was $110,000, which is how much she paid for it over ten years ago. She receives an insurance reimbursement of $185,000, which exceeds her basis in the home by $75,000. How many years does Edwina have to replace the home before she has to pay tax on the gain?

A. Two years.
B. Three years.
C. Four years.
D. She must pay tax on the gain because her primary residence does not qualify for an exclusion.

65. Charlotte is 17 years old and works part-time at a retail store. She is a high school student and is claimed by her parents as a qualifying child. During the year, she earned $6,500 in wages from her part-time job. She also had $5,200 in dividend income from stocks that she inherited from her grandfather. Is Charlotte required to file a tax return, and if so, why?

A. Charlotte is not required to file a tax return.
B. Charlotte is required to file a tax return because her unearned income is subject to the kiddie tax.
C. Charlotte is required to file a tax return because her gross income is above the standard deduction amount for qualifying children.
D. Charlotte is required to file a tax return because her income is above the gross income limits for qualifying relatives.

66. In 2023, the Lifetime Learning Credit is limited to $2,000 per:

A. Qualifying student.
B. Taxpayer.
C. Tax return.
D. Dependent.

67. Which of the following filing statuses would prevent a taxpayer from claiming a deduction for student loan interest?

A. Married Filing Separately.
B. Married Filing Jointly.
C. Single.
D. Head of Household.

68. Celeste is unmarried and 65 years old. She receives qualified Medicaid waiver payments for the personal care of her adult disabled son in her home. The Medicaid waiver payments total $17,000 for the year. Celeste also receives $12,000 in Social Security Income during the year. Does Celeste have to file a tax return in 2023?

A. She does not have to file a return because neither the Medicaid waiver payments nor the Social Security income are taxable.
B. She must file a return because the Medicaid waiver payments and the Social Security income are taxable.
C. She must file a return because the Social Security income is taxable.
D. She does not have to file a return because the Social Security income is taxable and below the standard deduction amount.

69. Nivaldo received a scholarship to attend the University of Denver. He decides to take three college courses, but he is not a degree candidate, and he drops out before completing his first year. The scholarship is for $5,000. Nivaldo's tuition was $3,000, and his books were $900. He had no other education expenses. How much of the scholarship is taxable to Nivaldo?

A. $0
B. $1,100
C. $2,000
D. $5,000

70. Kamden and Octavia are married and file jointly. They have a combined AGI of $78,000 in 2023. They have one daughter, age 17, and one son, age 16. They claim both their children as dependents. All of them are U.S. citizens and have lived in the U.S. the entire year. What is the maximum Child Tax Credit that Kamden and Octavia may be eligible for in 2023?

A. $2,000
B. $3,000
C. $4,000
D. $6,000

71. Rhett is unmarried and files as head of household. He has sole custody of his 7-year-old son, Jimmy, who he claims as his dependent. Rhett had the following items of income and loss in 2023:

| | |
|---|---|
| Form W-2 wage income | $42,000 |
| Gambling winnings | $2,000 |
| Gambling losses | ($4,000) |
| Dependent care FSA benefits from his employer | $3,000 |
| Capital loss carryover from the prior year | ($7,500) |

Rhett spent $3,200 on Jimmy's daycare during the year. He does not plan to itemize his deductions. Based on the information above, how much gross income must Rhett report on his tax return?

A. $36,500
B. $39,000
C. $41,000
D. $58,500

72. In general, royalties from copyrights, patents, oil, gas, and mineral properties are taxable as:

A. Capital gains.
B. Ordinary income.
C. Self-employment income.
D. Rental income.

73. Which of the following taxes are deductible on Schedule A as an itemized deduction?

A. Federal income tax.
B. State income tax.
C. Excise tax on alcohol and tobacco.
D. Real estate taxes on foreign property.

74. Abner and Viola are married. Viola is 65 and earned $18,400 in wages during the year. Abner is 62 years old and blind. He earned $5,400 in wages for the year. Abner also received $800 in HSA distributions in 2023, all of which were used for qualifying medical expenses. Are they required to file a tax return?

A. Their income is below the filing requirement, so they do not have to file a return.
B. Viola is required to file a tax return, but Abner is not.
C. Abner is required to file a tax return, but Viola is not.
D. They are required to file a tax return, whether they file jointly or separately.

75. Ignoring any income limitations, which of the following taxpayers would *not* be eligible for the refundable Additional Child Tax Credit?

A. A taxpayer who files head of household and claims a foster child that is three years of age.
B. A married couple that files jointly and claims their 10-year-old daughter.
C. A widowed taxpayer that has one 18-year-old child and one newborn that was born in 2023.
D. A taxpayer who files Form 2555 and elects to exclude foreign-earned income from tax.

76. All of the following income types are reported on Form 1099-MISC except:

A. Rents over $600.
B. Crop insurance proceeds over $600.
C. Canceled debt of $600 or more.
D. Royalty income over $10.

77. Which of the following taxpayers would *not* be able to file jointly in 2023?

A. A married couple with one spouse who is a nonresident alien.
B. A couple living together in a common-law marriage recognized in the state where they live.
C. A married couple who are separated under an interlocutory (not final) decree of divorce.
D. A couple whose marriage was annulled on January 12, 2024.

78. Keenan, a U.S. citizen, is married to Seraphina, a citizen of France. Seraphina's daughter from a prior marriage is a French citizen and does not have a green card. Keenan has not adopted his wife's daughter. They all live together in France. The child was not physically present in the U.S. during the tax year. Can Keenan claim his stepdaughter as a dependent?

A. Yes, Keenan can claim his stepdaughter as a dependent, providing he requests an ITIN for her.
B. Yes, Keenan can claim his stepdaughter as a dependent, and also file as head of household.
C. Keenan can claim his stepdaughter as a dependent, but only if he files jointly with his wife.
D. Keenan cannot claim his stepdaughter as a dependent.

79. Carla has one brother named Neal. On December 27, 2023, Neal dies, and Carla is the sole beneficiary of his estate. Neal was still owed accrued wages when he died. The employer issued the check directly to Carla the following year, on January 20, 2024. What is the tax consequence of Carla receiving wage income that was due to Neal at the time of his death?

A. The income is tax-free to Carla.
B. The income is ordinary income to Carla and reported to her on Form 1099-MISC.
C. The income is ordinary income to Carla and reported to her on Form W-2.
D. The income is a short-term capital gain for Carla.

80. Alexis sold land that she had purchased for investment purposes to her brother Samuel for $16,000. On the date of the sale, Alexis's basis in the land was $17,000, and she had owned the land for 14 months. Alexis cannot deduct the $1,000 loss because her brother is a related party. The land continues to decline in value, and six months later, Samuel sold the same land to an unrelated party for $15,500. What amount of loss can Samuel deduct on his tax return?

A. $0, because it is a related party sale
B. $500 long-term capital loss
C. $500 short-term capital loss
D. $1,500 long-term capital loss

81. Owen and Heloise are married and file jointly. On February 2, 2023, they invested in a mutual fund, purchasing 90,000 shares. On December 28, 2023, the mutual fund reported $22,000 of capital gains to their mutual fund account. However, only $5,000 was actually distributed to them in 2023. The rest was distributed in the following year, on January 4, 2024. What is the amount and nature of the capital gain they must report on their 2023 tax joint return?

A. $5,000 short-term capital gain.
B. $5,000 long-term capital gain.
C. $22,000 short-term capital gain.
D. $22,000 long-term capital gain.

82. Janet is a freelance editor who files a Schedule C. Janet operates her business on a cash basis. On December 14, 2023, she completed a project editing an author's novel. She billed the publisher $2,000 for the work on the same date. On December 26, 2023, the check arrived in Janet's mailbox. Her son collected it with the other mail because Janet was on vacation. Janet did not receive the check until she arrived back in town on January 5, 2024. She deposited the check on January 10, 2024. When must Janet recognize the income on her Schedule C?

A. 2023.
B. 2024.
C. Either 2023 or 2024.
D. Split equally between 2023 and 2024.

83. Which of the following taxpayers may claim the Section 199A qualified business income deduction?

A. Individuals, trusts, and estates on their qualified business income.
B. Individuals on their wage income.
C. Individuals, trusts, and estates on their interest income.
D. C Corporations with qualified business income.

84. Isaiah is a full-time life insurance salesman. His employer issued him a Form W-2, but Isaiah reports his wages and allowable expenses on Schedule C. He does not pay self-employment tax or file a Schedule SE. For federal tax purposes, Isaiah is considered a:

A. An independent contractor.
B. A statutory employee.
C. A statutory nonemployee.
D. A common-law employee.

85. Leif, age 61, made a traditional IRA contribution of $7,000 on January 10, 2023, intending the contribution to apply to the 2023 tax year. A month later, he unexpectedly loses his job. His total wages for 2023 were only $5,500. His state unemployment benefits totaled $16,600, and he had additional passive rental income of $36,000 from a residential rental property that he owns. Which of the following statements is correct about Leif's IRA contribution?

A. He has not made an excess contribution to his IRA, because he is over 50 and allowed to make a larger IRA contribution during the year.
B. He has made a $500 excess contribution to his IRA. He must correct the excess contribution, or he will have to pay an excise tax.
C. He has made a $1,500 excess contribution to his IRA. He must correct the excess contribution, or he will have to pay an excise tax.
D. He has made a $7,000 excess contribution to his IRA. He must correct the excess contribution, or he will have to pay an excise tax.

86. Brenda has five separate certificates of deposit (CDs) in five different banks. The total amount of interest she earned from the investments in 2023 is $4,500. Which form is she required to use to report this income?

A. Schedule A.
B. Schedule B.
C. Schedule C.
D. Schedule D.

87. Landry is an Army veteran. He was injured while serving in a combat zone and was later awarded Veterans Affairs (VA) disability severance benefits. In 2023, he received $1,679 per month in disability benefits. How should these payments be reported on Landry's tax return?

A. Up to 80% of the disability severance benefits may be excluded from income.
B. The disability benefits are excluded from income tax, but are still subject to Social Security tax.
C. The disability severance benefits are taxable as ordinary income.
D. All of the disability severance benefits may be excluded from income.

88. Minnie is a part-time substitute teacher at her local middle school. In 2023, she spent $185 on school supplies for her students. She also paid $190 for a professional development course to help her manage an online classroom. During the tax year, she has 440 hours of paid employment as an educator at the school. How much of her expenses can she deduct as an adjustment to income using the Educator Expense Deduction?

A. $0
B. $185
C. $250
D. $300

89. Kristine volunteered to work at her church's annual fundraiser, a rummage sale. She spent an entire weekend volunteering at the event. Which of the following donations are not allowed as a charitable contribution?

A. Fair market value of the hours she spent volunteering at the church's rummage sale.
B. Fair market value of used furniture, in good condition, that she donated to the sale.
C. Cash contribution to purchase office supplies for use during the rummage sale.
D. Her transportation expenses for driving to and from the church during the rummage sale.

90. Calder sells a plot of land with an adjusted basis of $100,000 in 2023. The buyer agrees to pay $125,000, with a cash down payment of $25,000 and $20,000 (plus 4% interest) in each of the next five years. What is Calder's gross profit on this installment sale, and what amount is taxable in 2023?

A. The gross profit is $5,000, and $5,000 is taxable in the current year.
B. The gross profit is $10,000, and $10,000 is taxable in the current year.
C. The gross profit is $25,000, and $2,000 is taxable in the current year.
D. The gross profit is $25,000, and $5,000 is taxable in the current year.

91. Emmett was injured in a train wreck three years ago and suffered serious physical injuries. After several years of litigation, he received a combined court settlement in 2023 that included reimbursement of his medical bills of $200,000, reimbursement of lost wages of $100,000, additional compensation of $450,000 for pain and suffering, and interest of $15,000. What portion of his court settlement is taxable?

A. $0
B. $15,000
C. $115,000
D. $450,000

92. Clarita is 45, unmarried, and files as Head of Household. Clarita fully supports her elderly mother, Nancy, who is age 85, disabled, and lives with her. In 2023, Clarita worked full-time and earned $72,000 in wages. She also received $8,000 of rental income from a residential rental. Clarita paid $5,600 to a home care agency for a part-time in-home caregiver to help take care of her mother while she was working. Clarita had job-based health insurance all year, and Nancy was enrolled in Medicare. Based on this information, which of the following credits will Clarita likely qualify for?

A. Child and Dependent Care Credit
B. Earned Income Tax Credit
C. Advanced Premium Tax Credit
D. Child Tax Credit

93. Morgaine is 16 years old. She lives with her parents and does not provide more than half of her own support. She inherited several investments from her grandmother when she died two years ago. In 2023, Morgaine had the following income:

| | |
|---|---|
| Wages from a part-time job | $4,000 |
| Dividends from investments | $3,300 |
| Taxable interest | $900 |
| Tax-exempt interest from muni bonds | $100 |
| Capital gains | $500 |
| Capital losses on the sale of stock | ($400) |

The dividends were qualified dividends on stock given to her by her grandmother. Is (1) Morgaine subject to the kiddie tax, and (2) what is her *unearned* income for 2023?

A. No. Her unearned income totals $700.
B. No. Her unearned income totals $1,000.
C. Yes. Her unearned income totals $4,300.
D. Yes. Her unearned income totals $4,800.

94. Rowan bought his home in 2015 and lived in it continuously for 2½ years. Starting on January 1, 2018, he was on qualified official extended duty in the U.S. Air Force, and he did not live in the home during that time. Instead, the house remained vacant. Rowan finally sold the home in 2023 and had a $42,000 gain on the sale. How should this gain be reported on his tax return?

A. He does not have to report the gain on the sale.
B. The gain should be reported as a long-term capital gain on Schedule D.
C. The gain should be reported as a short-term capital gain on Schedule D.
D. The gain should be reported as "other income" on Form 1040.

95. Tobias is a U.S. citizen serving in the Navy. He is stationed in the Philippines. His wife and children live with him, and his children, ages 6 and 10, are U.S. citizens and have valid Social Security numbers. Tobias is able to claim his children as dependents. Tobias's wife, Mayumi, is a citizen of the Philippines. She does not want to file jointly with Tobias and does not wish to be treated as a U.S. resident alien for tax purposes. Mayumi owns a successful business in the Philippines, and she does not want to report her worldwide income and pay tax on it. Which of the following statements is correct?

A. Tobias does not have to file a return until he comes back to the United States.
B. Tobias can file as head of household and claim his children as dependents.
C. Since Tobias is married and living with his spouse, he cannot claim head of household status. He must file as married filing separately.
D. Tobias can file jointly with his wife and sign on her behalf since his wife is a nonresident alien.

96. Which of the following scenarios is considered a passive activity and subject to the passive activity loss limitations?

A. Farming activity in which the taxpayer does not materially participate.
B. Rental activity in which the taxpayer is a real estate professional.
C. Royalties earned by a self-employed inventor.
D. Portfolio income earned from investments.

97. Roseanne is 65 and single. She received the following income during the year:

| | |
|---|---|
| Social Security benefits | $12,400 |
| Wage income | $92,000 |
| Capital gains from the sale of stock | $31,000 |

Based on this information, what is the *maximum* taxable amount of Roseanne's Social Security benefits?

A. $6,200
B. $10,540
C. $12,400
D. $25,000

98. Which of the following statements is **true** about the filing of FBAR and Form 8938?

A. Both FBAR and Form 8938 are filed with the FinCEN.
B. FBAR is filed with the IRS and Form 8938 is filed with the FinCEN.
C. FBAR is filed with the FinCEN and Form 8938 is filed with the IRS.
D. Both FBAR and Form 8938 are filed with the IRS.

99. Which of the following retirement plans offers tax-free growth and tax-free withdrawals?

A. Roth IRA
B. SIMPLE IRA
C. Traditional IRA
D. 401(k) plan

100. Sawyer died on March 20, 2023. Sawyer's last will named his attorney as his executor. His executor compiled the following information about Sawyer's assets and liabilities at the time of his death:

- Cash and investments of $6,325,000.
- Life insurance proceeds of $10,000,000, payable to his wife.
- Personal residence with FMV of $500,000, owned jointly with his wife, a U.S. citizen.
- Credit card debts of $200,000 that were owed at the time of Sawyer's death.

In addition, funeral expenses of $25,000 and $50,000 in attorney's fees were paid out of the estate. All of Sawyer's assets passed to his wife upon his death, according to his will. His wife is a U.S. citizen. Based upon the information above, what is the amount of Sawyer's taxable estate?

A. $0
B. $2,625,000
C. $2,550,000
D. $2,575,000

**Please review your answer choices with the correct answers in the next section.**

# Answers to Exam #2: Individuals

**1. The answer is A.** Heath has made an IRA-type distribution. A checkmark in the "IRA/SEP/SIMPLE" checkbox in box 7 of Form 1099-R indicates that the taxpayer received an IRA-type distribution. Since Heath is over the age of 59½, he can take distributions from his IRA without facing a 10 percent early distribution penalty, although he will owe income tax on the distribution, unless he rolls over his distribution within 60 days into another qualifying retirement plan.

| | | | |
|---|---|---|---|
| ☐ VOID ☐ CORRECTED | | | |

| PAYER'S name, street address, city or town, state or province, country, ZIP or foreign postal code, and telephone no.<br><br>ABC BUSINESS, INC.<br>123 MAIN ST.<br>LAS VEGAS, NV 89001 | **1** Gross distribution<br><br>$ $3,000<br>**2a** Taxable amount<br><br>$ | OMB No. 1545-0119<br><br>2023<br><br>Form **1099-R** | **Distributions From Pensions, Annuities, Retirement or Profit-Sharing Plans, IRAs, Insurance Contracts, etc.** |
| | **2b** Taxable amount not determined **X** | Total distribution ☐ | Copy 1<br>**For State, City, or Local Tax Department** |
| PAYER'S TIN<br>56-1223456 | RECIPIENT'S TIN<br>123-45-6789 | **3** Capital gain (included in box 2a)<br>$ | **4** Federal income tax withheld<br>$ | |
| RECIPIENT'S name<br><br>HEATH SMITH | **5** Employee contributions/ Designated Roth contributions or insurance premiums<br>$ | **6** Net unrealized appreciation in employer's securities<br>$ | |
| Street address (including apt. no.)<br>ONE FIRST ST. | **7** Distribution code(s)<br>7 | IRA/ SEP/ SIMPLE<br>**X** | **8** Other<br>$ % | |
| City or town, state or province, country, and ZIP or foreign postal code<br>LAS VEGAS, NV 98000 | **9a** Your percentage of total distribution %  | **9b** Total employee contributions<br>$ | |
| **10** Amount allocable to IRR within 5 years<br>$ | **11** 1st year of desig. Roth contrib. | **12** FATCA filing requirement ☐ | **14** State tax withheld<br>$<br>$ | **15** State/Payer's state no. | **16** State distribution<br>$<br>$ |
| Account number (see instructions)<br>987654321 | | **13** Date of payment | **17** Local tax withheld<br>$<br>$ | **18** Name of locality | **19** Local distribution<br>$<br>$ |

Form **1099-R**     www.irs.gov/Form1099R     Department of the Treasury - Internal Revenue Service

**2. The answer is D.** IRD is included in the decedent's estate and **may be subject to estate tax.** Income in respect of a decedent (IRD) is any taxable income that was *earned* but not *received* by the decedent by the time of death. IRD is not taxed on the final return of the deceased taxpayer. IRD is reported on the tax return of the person (or entity) that receives the income. This could be the estate, in which case, it would be reported on Form 1041. Otherwise, it could be the surviving spouse or another beneficiary, such as a child. If it is received by a beneficiary and subject to income tax on the beneficiary's return, the beneficiary can claim a deduction for any estate tax paid on the IRD. This deduction is taken as a miscellaneous itemized deduction on Schedule A and is *not* subject to the 2% floor, so it is fully deductible.

**3. The answer is C.** Everly cannot include the cost of health club dues.[18] Qualifying medical expenses *do not* include the cost of membership in any club organized for business, pleasure, recreation, or other social purpose, such as health club dues, private gym fees, or amounts paid for steam baths, spas, or retreats that are merely for general health or to relieve physical or mental discomfort not related to a particular medical condition. All the other expenses would be qualifying expenses.[19] Taxpayers should save receipts of their purchases for their records.

**4. The answer is D.** Victoria can claim **$26,400** in alimony paid as an adjustment to income on her Form 1040, the total of the medical expenses, and the regular alimony paid ($15,000 + $11,400). The payer can deduct the full amount if it is required by the divorce agreement or divorce decree. Since Victoria's divorce decree included a written stipulation that she was required to pay her ex-spouse's ongoing medical expenses, then those payments would also qualify as alimony. Alimony is a payment to or for a former spouse under a divorce or separation agreement. Alimony does not include voluntary payments that are not made under a divorce or separation decree. Payments to a third party (such as the payment directly to the hospital) on behalf of an ex-spouse under the terms of a divorce agreement can qualify as alimony. These include payments for an ex-spouse's medical expenses, housing costs (rent, utilities, etc.), taxes, and tuition. The payments are treated as received by the spouse and then paid to the third party.

> **Note:** The Tax Cuts and Jobs Act (TCJA) permanently eliminated the deduction for alimony payments starting in 2019. However, divorce judgments that were finalized *before* 2019 (December 31, 2018, and earlier) are considered "grandfathered," and the old rules (which allowed for a deduction for the payor and required the recipient to recognize taxable income) normally apply.

**5. The answer is A.** Prescott can only contribute **$5,200**, the amount of his qualifying compensation for the year. For 2023, a taxpayer's total contributions to all traditional and Roth IRAs cannot be more than $6,500 (or $7,500 if the taxpayer is age 50 or older). However, these amounts are also limited by the taxpayer's "qualifying compensation." Qualifying compensation is generally earned income, including wages or self-employment income. Nontaxable combat pay and taxable alimony are also considered earned income for IRA purposes. Passive income, such as rental income, interest income, unemployment payments, and Social Security benefits, do not qualify as "compensation" for making an IRA contribution. Since Prescott's only qualifying compensation is his wages, his IRA contribution would be limited to that amount.

---

[18] A taxpayer cannot include in medical expenses the cost of health club dues or any weight-loss program if the purpose of the weight loss is the improvement of appearance, general health, or sense of well-being. A taxpayer cannot include amounts incurred to lose weight unless the weight loss is a treatment for a specific disease diagnosed by a physician (such as obesity, hypertension, or heart disease).

[19] The CARES Act modified the rules that apply to various tax-advantaged accounts (HSAs, Archer MSAs, Health FSAs, and HRAs) so that additional items are "qualified medical expenses" that may be reimbursed from those accounts. Specifically, the cost of menstrual care products and over-the-counter medications are now reimbursable through a health savings account (even without a prescription).

**6. The answer is A.** Sloane has not made a qualifying charitable contribution. The value of the "free use" of a taxpayer's property is not allowed as a charitable deduction. Qualified contributions must be made in cash or property.

**7. The answer is C.** Wilson's office is 20% (240 ÷ 1,200) of the total area of his home. Therefore, his business percentage is 20%. His year-end expenses were $12,000 in rent ($1,000 per month × 12 months) and $600 in utilities ($50 × 12 months). The answer is calculated as follows:

$12,000 total rent

$600 total utilities

$12,600 total expenses for the year × 20% (business-use percentage) = **$2,520.**

> **Note:** The amount above, using the "actual expense" method, is more than the $1,200 amount using the simplified safe harbor method of $5.00 per square foot of office space. In this case, using actual costs will generate a larger deduction for Wilson. The home office deduction is figured on Form 8829, *Expenses for Business Use of Your Home.*

**8. The answer is C.** Clarence's qualifying medical expenses are $5,100 for the year ($2,300 + $1,200 + $1,100 + $500). Health club dues and medical marijuana are not qualifying medical expenses, so those expenses are not included in the calculation. In this example, Clarence could deduct **$2,100** of his medical expenses because $2,100 is the amount of qualifying medical expenses that exceeds 7.5% of his AGI ($40,000 AGI × 7.5% = $3,000). To review a full list of qualifying medical expenses, see Publication 502, Medical and Dental Expenses.

**9. The answer is D.** Sebastian is Olivia's qualifying child for Head of Household and EITC purposes. Although he does not meet the "age test" for EITC, he is permanently disabled, so he is still considered a "qualifying child" for EITC purposes despite his age. Since Sebastian does not provide more than one-half of his own support, he can be claimed as a dependent on Olivia's tax return. And Olivia also qualified as HOH because she pays the costs of keeping up the home where her son, Sebastian, resides. See Publication 596, *Earned Income Credit,* for more information and similar scenarios.

**10. The answer is A.** Laureen can deduct any jury duty pay remitted to her employer as an adjustment to income on Schedule 1 of Form 1040. Many employers (including most large employers and government agencies) have a policy that compensates employees for any time spent on jury service. Sometimes an employer will continue to pay an employee their regular salary while the employee serves on a jury. If employers do continue to pay the employee's salary, the employer has the right to require the employee to remit to them the fees received for jury service. The employee can then deduct the amount remitted as an adjustment to their income.

**11. The answer is B.** Elijah's adjusted gross income is calculated as follows:

| | |
|---|---|
| W-2 Wages (Job #1) | $5,000 |
| W-2 Wages (Job #2) | $18,500 |
| Gross wages | $23,500 |
| Subtract allowable capital loss (limited to $3,000) | ($3,000) |
| Gross income | $20,500 |
| Early withdrawal penalty | ($130) |
| **Adjusted gross income** | **$20,370** |

Elijah's allowable capital loss limit is $3,000 per return ($1,500 for MFS). Individuals can deduct up to $3,000 of net capital losses against noncapital gain income. This allowable capital loss is subtracted from total gross wages to determine gross income. Any amount above the $3,000 threshold must be carried over to future years (Elijah has a $1,000 capital loss carryover). The early withdrawal penalty is allowed as an adjustment to income to arrive at adjusted gross income (AGI).

**12. The answer is D.** Julie can file a Form 706 in order to elect portability of the DSUE amount. When a surviving spouse wants to benefit from the deceased spouse's unused exclusion (DSUE), they must file Form 706. By doing so, they can carry over the unused portion of the decedent's estate tax exclusion to their own estate, potentially reducing future estate taxes. This election allows the surviving spouse to use both their own exclusion and the DSUE amount for estate tax purposes.

**13. The answer is B.** Living in a federally declared disaster area will qualify a taxpayer for an automatic filing extension. Taxpayers who find themselves in a federally declared disaster area (due to natural disasters like hurricanes, floods, or wildfires) qualify for a postponement of time to file returns, pay taxes and perform other time-sensitive acts.

**14. The answer is D.** Blakely's main home is her rental apartment in Salt Lake City because she lives and works there *most of the time.*[20] If she were to sell the ski condo in Park City, she would *not* qualify for the section 121 exclusion on the sale because it is a vacation home and not her primary residence (unless she were to own and have previously used the condo as her primary residence for at least two years in the five years preceding its sale).

**15. The answer is C.** Arthur can claim a $4,000 Child Tax Credit in 2023 ($2,000 per child). For tax year 2023, taxpayers claiming the Child Tax Credit can receive up to $2,000 per qualifying child under the age of 17. The maximum Child Tax Credit in 2023 is available to taxpayers with a modified adjusted gross income of $200,000 or below ($400,000 for MFJ).

---

[20] Generally, a taxpayer's "main home" is the home that the taxpayer spends most of their time. The IRS allows taxpayers to designate one residence only as a "main home" at any one time.

**16. The answer is A.** The custodial parent is the parent with whom the child lived for the greater number of nights during the year. The other parent is the noncustodial parent. If the parents divorced or separated during the year and the child lived with both parents before the separation, the custodial parent is the one with whom the child lived for the greater number of nights during the rest of the year. If the child lived with each parent for an equal number of nights during the year, the custodial parent is the parent with the higher adjusted gross income.

> **Note**: If a child is emancipated under state law, the child is treated as independent and not having lived with either parent.

**17. The answer is D.** In Skylar's case, since her funds in her foreign accounts totaled $52,000 on the last day of the tax year, she is required to file both Form 8938, *Statement of Specified Foreign Financial Assets,* and an FBAR. There are two separate reporting requirements that may apply to taxpayers who hold certain types of foreign assets or who have certain amounts of funds in foreign bank accounts. An FBAR generally must be filed with the Treasury Department if a taxpayer has more than $10,000 in offshore bank accounts. Taxpayers also must file a Form 8938 with the IRS if they hold foreign financial assets with an aggregate value that exceeds $50,000 ($100,000 MFJ) on the last day of the tax year, or that exceeds $75,000 ($150,000 MFJ) at any time during the tax year.

> **Note**: The due date for FBAR filings is generally April 15, consistent with the Federal income tax due date, but there is an automatic extension to file the FBAR until October 15.

**18. The answer is A**. Wesley does not have to report Social Security and Medicare taxes on the nanny's wages. If an employer pays a **household employee** less than $2,600 in wages in 2023, the employer does not have to report and pay Social Security and Medicare taxes on that employee's wages. As long as the amount is less than this threshold, the taxpayer is not required to withhold or pay employment taxes or provide the employee with Form W-2. However, the wages are still taxable to the nanny for income tax purposes and must be reported on her own tax return. If a taxpayer pays wages to a household employee that are above the reporting threshold, they will be required to file Schedule H, *Household Employment Taxes.* This form is submitted along with the taxpayer's individual Form 1040. For more information, see IRS Publication 926, *Household Employer's Tax Guide.*

**19. The answer is B.** Since this is a foreign adoption, Carter and Melissa may claim all $12,000 in qualified adoption expenses ($3,000 paid in 2021, $4,000 paid in 2022, and $5,000 in 2023) on their 2023 tax return, because 2023 is the year when the adoption becomes final.[21]

---

[21] A "foreign" adoption is the adoption of a child who is not a U.S. citizen or U.S. resident before the adoption process begins. Qualified adoption expenses paid before and during a foreign adoption are allowable as a credit for the year when the adoption becomes final. This question is based directly on an example in IRS Tax Topics 607, *Adoption Credit and Adoption Assistance Programs,* available at: https://www.irs.gov/taxtopics/tc607.

**20. The answer is B.** Laurent's gross estate will be valued either on the date of death, or (if eligible) six months after the date of death, if the executor chooses to use the alternate valuation date. If a taxpayer dies on March 18, 2023, the alternate valuation date is **September 18, 2023** (exactly six months later).

**21. The answer is C.** Willow's basis in the land is figured as follows:

| Donor's original basis | $8,700 |
|---|---|
| Add demolition costs | $3,200 |
| **Ending Basis** | **$11,900** |

In general, for purposes of determining gain, a taxpayer generally takes a "transferred basis" when they receive property as a gift when the fair market value at the time of the gift is greater than the donor's basis. This means that the donee's basis in the property is the same as the donor's basis. Demolition costs *increase* the basis of land, so the cost to demolish the foundation would be added to Willow's basis.

**22. The answer is B.** For IRA contributions, Josiah may contribute at any time during the year and up until April 15, 2024[22] (the filing deadline for 2023 individual returns). Filing an extension does not extend the IRA contribution deadline. Even after Josiah files his individual tax return, he can still contribute to an IRA, as long as the contribution is made no later than the unextended filing deadline. However, if Josiah fails to make his IRA contribution by the unextended filing deadline, he must file a Form 1040-X to amend the original return.

**23. The answer is B.** Foreign source income originates from a foreign country, whereas U.S. source income originates from the United States. Taxpayers must be able to distinguish between the two, since income earned in foreign countries can potentially be excluded from U.S. income tax up to a certain threshold. U.S. citizens and U.S. residents are subject to worldwide U.S. taxation on income from all sources.

**24. The answer is C.** Caroline and Xavier owe **$891** in Additional Medicare Tax, figured as follows: ($349,000 - $250,000 = $99,000 × .009 = **$891**). The Additional Medicare Tax of 0.9% is applied to their combined earned income ($155,000 + $18,000 + $176,000 = $349,000) above the threshold for a taxpayer's filing status. Caroline's court settlement is not taxable because it is for an injury or illness. Caroline and Xavier must file Form 8959, *Additional Medicare Tax,* to compute any Additional Medicare Tax due. Employers are required to withhold the Additional Medicare Tax if the individual is paid more than $200,000, regardless of the individual's filing status. Since Caroline and Xavier both earn under that threshold, they may request additional withholding by their employers (or make estimated tax payments).

---

[22] Taxpayers residing in Maine or Massachusetts have until April 17, 2024, because of the Patriots' Day and Emancipation Day holidays in those states. The extended deadline is October 15, 2024.

**25. The answer is B.** Marley's net investment income is $36,000, the total of his capital gains, rental income, and dividend income. Marley's MAGI exceeds the threshold for single filers by $71,000 ($271,000 - $200,000). Since $36,000 is less than $71,000, $36,000 is the amount on which the net investment income tax would be calculated ($36,000 × 3.8% = **$1,368**). For individuals, a 3.8% tax is imposed on the *lesser* of:

- The individual's net investment income for the year, or
- Any excess of the individual's modified adjusted gross income for the tax year over certain thresholds.

Net investment income does not include earned income, such as wages or self-employment earnings. Retirement income is also not included in net investment income, so the traditional IRA distributions would not be included in the calculation.

**26. The answer is B.** Leilani is allowed to take a portion of the rental losses based on her income, but her deduction is limited. The special allowance is limited to **$12,500** for married individuals who file MFS, but *only* if they lived apart from their spouses during the entire tax year. For married taxpayers who live together for any portion of the year and file separately, the rental losses are completely disallowed in the current year and must be carried forward. Since Leilani lives apart from her spouse, she is allowed 50% of the "special rental loss allowance," which is generally $25,000.

**27. The answer is D.** Lennox is allowed to roll over his traditional IRA into a 401(k) plan. Taxpayers are allowed to roll over their traditional IRA to any of the following plans without incurring tax or penalty:

- A rollover into another traditional IRA
- A qualified plan, like a 401(k) or 403(b)
- A tax-sheltered annuity plan
- A government deferred compensation plan

Although a traditional IRA can be *converted* to a Roth IRA, the taxable amount that is converted is added to the taxpayer's income and would be taxed as ordinary income.

> **Note**: IRAs cannot be held jointly, so spouses are not allowed to roll over funds into each other's retirement plans. However, a taxpayer is allowed to roll over an *inherited* IRA from a deceased spouse. After death, a surviving spouse may elect to treat the IRA as his or her own and roll it over into another traditional IRA.

**28. The answer is C.** Only the amount that exceeds the value of the benefit received (the dinner) would be deductible as a charitable gift. Therefore, Madeline must deduct the value of the dinners ($20 × 6 tickets = $120) from the amount she paid. The answer is **$160** ($280 - $120 = $160).

**29. The answer is A.** Landon can deduct the interest on all his mortgage loans on Schedule A. Under the Tax Cuts and Jobs Act (TCJA), there is no longer any deduction for interest on home equity loans, *unless* the home equity loan was used to "acquire, construct, or substantially improve" the home. Since Landon used the home equity loan to substantially improve the property by adding a new bedroom, he may deduct the interest on Schedule A as mortgage interest.

**30. The answer is D.** The maximum amount of investment income that Joshua can have and still claim the Earned Income Tax Credit is $11,000 in 2023. The American Rescue Plan Act substantially increased the amount of investment income a taxpayer can receive and still be eligible for the EITC.

**31. The answer is C.** Robin's transportation and travel costs are not qualifying expenses for a Section 529 plan. Section 529 plans can be used for qualified educational expenses, including: tuition (including tuition at an elementary or secondary public or private school and higher education, such as colleges and technical schools), required books, computer equipment, school supplies, and room and board. The SECURE Act of 2019 also allows a distribution of up to $10,000 (total, not annually) to be applied to any qualified student loan.

**32. The answer is A.** Talia cannot deduct her IRA contribution. She must designate this contribution as a nondeductible contribution, because she was already covered by a workplace retirement plan and her modified AGI was over $83,000 in 2023. She cannot *deduct* the traditional IRA contribution. She must designate her contribution as a nondeductible contribution by reporting it on Form 8606, *Nondeductible IRAs.* For 2023, the maximum combined traditional IRA deduction or Roth contribution is $6,500 ($7,500 if age 50 or older). For taxpayers who are **already covered** by a retirement plan at work, the deduction for contributions to a traditional IRA is reduced (phased out) if the taxpayer's MAGI is:

- More than $116,000 but less than $136,000 for MFJ or QSS
- More than $73,000 but less than $83,000 for an individual filing as Single, HOH, or MFS and did not live with the spouse at any time during the year.
- Less than $10,000 for a married individual filing MFS who lived with their spouse.

**33. The answer is D.** Weston is not required to take minimum distributions from his Roth IRA.[23] Unlike traditional IRAs, Roth IRA accounts are not subject to required minimum distributions. Distributions would only be required after Weston dies (by the beneficiary of the account).

---

[23] Roth IRAs do not require RMDs, but traditional IRAs do. RMD rules apply to traditional IRAs, Simple IRAs and defined contribution plans (e.g., 401(k), profit-sharing, and 403(b) plans).

**34. The answer is C.** Only certain expenses are deductible as medical expenses on Schedule A. The answer is figured as follows:

| Expense | Amount |
|---|---|
| Vitamins for general health | Not deductible |
| Prescription medications imported from Canada | Not deductible |
| Hearing aids for Wesson | $320 |
| Prescription eyeglasses | $1,000 |
| Chiropractor fees | $4,400 |
| Acupuncture | $1,250 |
| **Qualifying medical expenses** | **$6,970** |

To review a full list of qualifying medical expenses, see Publication 502, *Medical and Dental Expenses.*

**35. The answer is D.** The stock is restricted, so Faith does not have constructive receipt of it. She should not report any taxable income until she receives the stock without restrictions. "Constructive receipt" does not require physical possession of the item of income. However, there are substantial restrictions on the stock's disposition, because Faith must complete another two years of service before she can sell or otherwise dispose of the stock.

**36. The answer is C.** Neither Ezra nor Dawn is eligible for the American Opportunity Credit, because they are in graduate school, and both had previously completed four years of postsecondary studies. The AOTC applies only to the first four years of postsecondary studies. The Lifetime Learning Credit is easy to calculate because it is based on 20% credit for up to $10,000 in allowable expenses ($10,000 × 20% = $2,000 maximum credit). Since Ezra and Dawn have $11,700 ($4,800 + $6,900) in qualified education expenses (which is more than the maximum allowed of $10,000), their credit is **$2,000.**

**37. The answer is B.** Paloma's deduction for State and Local Taxes is limited to $5,000 on Schedule A. In 2023, a taxpayer's total allowable deduction for state and local income, sales and property taxes is limited to a combined total deduction of $10,000, but only $5,000 if Married Filing Separately. Any state and local taxes she paid above this amount cannot be deducted on Schedule A. This is commonly called the "SALT cap." Under the Tax Cuts and Jobs Act, the deduction for state and local income taxes is limited to $10,000 ($5,000 for MFS). The SALT Cap applies for tax years through 2025, unless Congress decides to change it.

> **Note:** If Paloma's husband did *not* plan to itemize, then she would be forced to take the standard deduction, or else claim *zero* in itemized deductions, even if she would have otherwise had deductions to itemize on Schedule A.

**38. The answer is A.** In the year a taxpayer dies, if the surviving spouse does *not* remarry, the deceased spouse can use either MFJ or MFS. However, since Tasha remarried before the end of the year, the only filing status available to Bryan is "Married Filing Separately." Bryan's executor (Nolan, the attorney) would be responsible for filing any outstanding tax returns.

**39. The answer is D.** If Greg deposits an amount equal to the gross distribution into an IRA within the next 60 days, he will not be required to pay taxes on the money or be penalized for the mistake. This is called an "indirect rollover" or a "60-day rollover." Taxpayers are limited to one indirect rollover into a particular IRA every year (trustee-to-trustee transfers are not limited). The 60-day rollover rule applies to indirect rollovers of all or a portion of the assets in a qualified retirement account, such as a traditional IRA or 401(k). The taxpayer will receive a Form 1099-R to report the distribution and a Form 5498. They must report the indirect rollover on Form 1040 in order to avoid the tax.

**40. The answer is B.** Diallo and Hadiza would not qualify for EITC, because Hadiza does not have a valid Social Security number. **Both** spouses on a joint return must have valid Social Security numbers in order to qualify for EITC. None of the other scenarios would automatically disqualify a taxpayer from claiming EITC. Answer "A" is incorrect because a foster child is a qualifying child for EITC purposes. Answer "C" is incorrect because a taxpayer with no dependents can still qualify for EITC. Answer "D" is incorrect because earning income from a foreign country will not automatically disqualify a taxpayer from claiming EITC. Taxpayers that file Form 2555, *Foreign Earned Income,* do not qualify for the Earned Income Tax Credit.

**41. The answer is C.** If Axel claims a deduction for a charitable contribution of noncash property worth more than $5,000, he is required to obtain a qualified appraisal and must fill out Form 8283, *Noncash Charitable Contributions.* All of the other contributions would be deductible and fulfill the IRS' recordkeeping requirements for charitable gifts.

**42. The answer is A.** Nikos and Heather can *each* make a maximum contribution of $6,500 to a traditional IRA in 2023. This is because Nikos, who has no compensation, can include Heather's compensation to figure his maximum contribution to a traditional IRA. This special rule is only available to married taxpayers who file jointly. If Nikos had filed MFS, then he would not be allowed to contribute to an IRA, since he did not have any qualifying compensation. Because they are under the age of 50, they can contribute a maximum of $6,500 each in 2023 (taxpayers age 50 and older get an additional catch-up contribution of $1,000).

**43. The answer is C.** The rebate is not taxable. Reuben would reduce his basis in the car by $2,000. A cash rebate received from a dealer or manufacturer of an item is not taxable, but the taxpayer must reduce his basis by the amount of the rebate (based on an example in Publication 17).

**44. The answer is B.** There is no "gross income test" with regard to a qualifying child. There is a "gross income test" for the determination of a qualifying *relative*, which is a different type of dependency relationship. In general, to be a taxpayer's *qualifying child*, the dependent must satisfy four tests:

- **Relationship test:** The dependent must be the taxpayer's child or stepchild (whether by blood or adoption), foster child, sibling or step-sibling, or a descendant of one of these.
- **Residency test:** The child has the same principal residence as the taxpayer for more than half the year. Exceptions apply for children of divorced or separated parents, kidnapped children, temporary absences, and for children who were born or died during the year.
- **Age test:** The child must be either younger than 19 years old, or be a student younger than 24, or permanently disabled of any age.
- **Support test:** The child did not provide more than one-half of their own support for the year.

> **Note:** You must understand the differences between a "qualifying relative" and a "qualifying child" for the EA Exam. A "qualifying child" may enable a taxpayer to claim several tax benefits, such as head of household filing status, the Child Tax Credit, the Child and Dependent Care Credit, and the Earned Income Tax Credit.

**45. The answer is D.** Victor has a $1,000 short-term capital loss and a $7,200 ($5,200 + $2,000) long-term capital gain. The loss on the sale of the Abbot Inc. stock is short-term because he owned the stock for less than a year. The gain on the sale of the empty lot is long-term gain, because inherited property is *always* treated as long-term property, regardless of how long the beneficiary holds the property. The gain on the sale of the Acutrim Inc. stock is also long-term gain because Victor held the stock for over a year.

**46. The answer is C.** Audrey's total itemized deduction for taxes is **$6,400** ($2,000 + $1,900 + $100 + $2,400 = $6,400). The $250 homeowners' association fee and the foreign property taxes (on the condo in Mexico) are not deductible. The Tax Cuts and Jobs Act eliminated the deduction for foreign real property taxes unless they are paid or accrued in carrying on a trade or business or in an activity engaged in for profit. All the other taxes are deductible on Schedule A, up to a $10,000 limit ($5,000 for MFS).

**47. The answer is C.** Tyson's parents cannot claim him as a dependent. Tyson cannot be claimed as a qualifying child, because he is not a full-time student. For IRS purposes, a full-time student must be enrolled in a qualifying degree or certificate program at least 5 months of the year. Since Tyson only attended college for three months before dropping out, he is not a full-time student. Tyson's parents cannot claim him as a qualifying relative because he made more than the "deemed personal exemption" amount of $4,700 in 2023. The "deemed exemption" is the amount used for purposes of determining who is a "qualifying relative" under IRC Sec. 152(d)(1)(B).

**48. The answer is A.** Felicity meets the support test because she did not provide half of her own support. The support test determines the level of support by the child, not the person who wants to claim the child as a dependent. A person's own funds are not counted as support unless they are *actually spent* for support. Since Felicity's income was deposited into a trust fund for college, it is not figured in the support calculation. Therefore, Felicity's parents can claim their daughter as a dependent on their return. Minor children generally do not provide more than half of their own support during the tax year.

**49. The answer is C.** Amounts contributed to Jayden's FSA are not subject to employment taxes or federal income taxes. FSAs are usually funded through voluntary salary reduction agreements with an employer, and employers and employees may both contribute. Healthcare flexible spending arrangements (FSAs) allow employees to be reimbursed for medical expenses on a pre-tax basis. Unlike HSAs, for which contributions must be reported on Form 1040, there are no reporting requirements for FSAs on a taxpayer's individual return.

**50. The answer is A.** Wade's son, Linus, is a qualifying child. A U.S. citizen's child is usually a U.S. citizen by birth, even if the child is born in another country.

**51. The answer is B.** Property taxes paid on a personal residence are an itemized deduction, only deductible on Schedule A. The other answers are all deductions that are allowed as adjustments to income on Form 1040 if the taxpayer otherwise qualifies to take the deduction.[24]

**52. The answer is B.** Serenity must recognize **$78,000** of short-term capital gain. The answer is figured as follows:

| Purchase price (Serenity's cost basis) | $239,000 |
|---|---|
| Add land-clearing expenditures | $12,000 |
| Adjusted basis | $251,000 |
| Sale price - basis ($329,000 - $251,000) = Gain on sale | **$78,000** |

Grading, land clearing, and demolition costs must be added to the basis of the land. In this case, Serenity's intent to build a home is not relevant. The nature of the gain is short-term because Serenity held the property for less than one year before she sold it.

**53. The answer is D.** A "recovery" is a refund or return of an amount for which a taxpayer deducted or took a credit in an earlier year. A taxpayer must include a recovery in income in the year he receives it, to the extent the deduction or credit reduced his tax in the earlier year. Refunds of federal income taxes are never included in a taxpayer's income because they are not allowed as a deduction.

---

[24] Alimony paid is only deductible as an adjustment to income if the divorce decree or support agreement was finalized before January 1, 2019.

**54. The answer is A.** The distribution from the estate would be reported to Kenzie on **Schedule K-1 (Form 1041)**. Nonpassive distributions would be reported on Kenzie's **Schedule E (Form 1040)**. How a taxpayer reports distributions from an estate depends on the character of the income in the hands of the estate. Each item of income retains the same character as it passes through to the individual. For example, if the income distributed includes dividends, tax-exempt interest, or capital gains, it would retain the same character in the hands of the beneficiary. Business income and other nonpassive income that is distributed from an estate would be reported on Part III of the taxpayer's Schedule E (Form 1040). The estate's personal representative (executor) should provide a Schedule K-1 (Form 1041) to each beneficiary who receives a distribution from the estate. The executor must furnish Schedule K-1 to each beneficiary by the date on which Form 1041 is due (including extensions).

**55. The answer is D.** All of the charges are deductible as mortgage interest, so Fletcher and Samantha's deduction is **$14,370** ($12,200 + $50 + $120 + $2,000). Taxpayers can deduct a late payment charge on a mortgage loan as mortgage interest. Sometimes, if a person pays off his home mortgage early, they must pay a prepayment penalty. The taxpayer can deduct a prepayment penalty as home mortgage interest, provided the penalty is not for a specific service performed or cost incurred in connection with the mortgage loan. When taxpayers sell their home, they can deduct home mortgage interest paid up to, but *not including*, the date of the sale.

**56. The answer is A.** Yousef's self-employment income is $185,000 for the year. The threshold amount for MFS filers is $125,000 for the calculation of the Additional Medicare Tax. Because Yousef's self-employment earnings exceed $125,000 (the threshold for MFS), Yousef will owe the additional 0.9% Medicare tax on $60,000 ($185,000 - $125,000). The Additional Medicare Tax due is **$540** ($60,000 × 0.9%). The rental income is not subject to the Additional Medicare Tax, so that income is not included in the calculation. Yousef will be required to remit the additional tax when he files his individual tax return. Yousef must file Form 8959, *Additional Medicare Tax,* to compute any Additional Medicare Tax due. A taxpayer is liable for Additional Medicare Tax if the taxpayer's *wages* or *self-employment income* (together with that of his or her spouse if filing a joint return) exceeds the threshold amount for the individual's filing status:

| Filing Status | Threshold Amount |
|---|---|
| Married filing jointly | $250,000 |
| Married filing separate | $125,000 |
| Single, HOH, Qualifying Surviving Spouse (QSS) | $200,000 |

**Note:** The *Additional Medicare Tax* was legislated as part of the Affordable Care Act. This tax was not repealed by the TCJA. Under this mandate, in addition to withholding Medicare tax at 1.45%, employers must withhold a 0.9% Additional Medicare Tax from an employee's wages once their earnings reach $200,000 in a calendar year.

**57. The answer is A.** Priscilla does not have to report the rental income. There is a special rule for homes that are rented for fewer than 15 days a year. In this case, the rental income is not taxable and does not need to be reported. A taxpayer's home can be rented out for less than 15 days each year without the need to report the rental income. This is the *"de minimis rental"* rule (also called the "15-day rule"). In this scenario, the house is still considered the taxpayer's personal residence, so the owner can deduct mortgage interest and property taxes on Schedule A as they normally would. Any rental expenses that Priscilla incurred would not be deductible.

**58. The answer is C.** Although Lenny owned the ten shares he received as a nontaxable stock dividend for only three months, all the stock has a long-term holding period. Stock acquired as a stock dividend has the same holding period as the original stock owned. Because he bought the stock for $1,500 three years ago, his holding period is long-term. Lenny has a long-term capital gain of **$530** on the sale of the 510 shares.

**59. The answer is B.** The student loan interest deduction is an adjustment to income in 2023. A taxpayer does not have to itemize expenses in order to claim a deduction for student loan interest that was paid during the year. The maximum amount that a taxpayer can deduct in 2023 as an adjustment to income is $2,500. This limit is the same for unmarried and joint filers. Taxpayers who file MFS cannot take the student loan interest deduction.

**60. The answer is D.** Antoinette must file a Schedule C for her store showing her net profit of $25,000, and Marty must file his own Schedule C for the carpentry business showing his net loss of $1,500. Antoinette's Schedule SE will show total earnings subject to SE tax of $25,000. Even if taxpayers file a joint return, they cannot file a "joint" Schedule SE. This is true whether one spouse or both spouses have earnings subject to self-employment tax. Married taxpayers cannot use losses from each other's businesses to offset self-employment tax. However, if an individual taxpayer operates multiple businesses, he would combine the net profit (or loss) from each to determine total earnings subject to SE tax. A loss from one business offsets the profit from another business. For example, if Antoinette had been running *both* businesses, the loss from the second business would have reduced her overall profit and also her self-employment tax.

**61. The answer is B.** Even though Porter is on Medicare, Norah may be eligible for a PTC if she enrolls in Marketplace coverage and is otherwise eligible based on household income (and other Marketplace requirements). Answer "A" is incorrect because Norah would not be disqualified from claiming the Premium Tax Credit or obtaining Marketplace coverage simply because her spouse was enrolled in Medicare. Answer "C" is incorrect because Norah does not have to file a separate return from her spouse in order to qualify for the Premium Tax Credit. Answer "D" is incorrect because only Norah would be able to qualify for the Premium Tax Credit. Porter already has Medicare coverage, so he is disqualified from claiming the credit. A person who is eligible for Medicare loses eligibility for PTC even if he or she fails to enroll in Medicare. See Publication 974, *Premium Tax Credit (PTC)*, for details.

**62. The answer is C.** Tucker must report $16,000 (his wages) plus $20,000, his lottery winnings ($16,000 + $20,000 = $36,000). The *worker's compensation* payments are not taxable and do not have to be reported on the return. Workers' compensation is a form of insurance, providing wage replacement and medical benefits to employees who are injured on the job.

**63. The answer is B.** Easton must include $200 in his 2023 taxable income. Although the reimbursement amount was $500, the only amount that has to be included in Easton's 2023 taxable income is $200—the amount he actually deducted (this question is based on an example in Publication 17, in the section on "itemized deduction recoveries").

**64. The answer is C.** Edwina has up to four years to replace her main home under the section 1033 rules for involuntary conversions. For an involuntary conversion in a <u>federally declared disaster area</u>, the taxpayer has up to <u>four years</u> after the end of the tax year in which any gain is realized to replace her principal residence (rather than the normal two-year replacement period) or to pay tax on any gain. Real property that is held for investment or used in a trade or business (such as a residential rental property or a commercial building) is allowed a three-year replacement period. The replacement period is generally four years for livestock involuntarily converted because of weather-related conditions.

**65. The answer is B.** Charlotte is required to file a tax return because her unearned income is subject to the kiddie tax. Children under age 18 and certain older children who are required to file a tax return and have unearned income over $2,500 in 2023 are required to file a return. In Charlotte's case, she must file Form 1040 and attach Form 8615, *Tax for Certain Children Who Have Unearned Income.*[25] Charlotte's wages will be taxed at her normal income tax rate, but her *unearned* income (the dividends) over the kiddie tax threshold is subject to the kiddie tax and will be taxed at her parents' marginal tax rate rather than her individual tax rate.

**66. The answer is C.** The Lifetime Learning Credit is limited to $2,000 *per tax return*. The credit is calculated as 20% of the first $10,000 of qualifying costs, regardless of the number of qualifying students, with a maximum credit of $2,000 ($10,000 × .20). The Lifetime Learning Credit can be used for a student who is not eligible for the American Opportunity Credit. However, a taxpayer cannot claim both the American Opportunity Credit and the Lifetime Learning Credit for the same student on the same return.

**67. The answer is A.** Taxpayers who file MFS (married filing separately) cannot claim the deduction for student loan interest. None of the other filing statuses listed would prevent a taxpayer from claiming the deduction.

---

[25] The kiddie tax applies to most unearned income, but doesn't apply to any salary or wages earned by the child, which is taxed at the child's ordinary rate. The kiddie tax does not apply if both of the child's parents are deceased, if the child independently provides more than one-half of their own support, or if the child files a joint return with a spouse.

**68. The answer is A.** Celeste does not have to file a return because she only has Social Security income. Medicaid waiver payments are excludable from gross income and do not need to be reported on the taxpayer's return.[26] However, Medicaid waiver payments can be considered earned income even though they are not taxable income. She may choose to file a return in order to receive a refund or any credits that she may be eligible for.

**69. The answer is D.** The full amount of the $5,000 scholarship is taxable to Nivaldo, because if a student is not a degree candidate, all scholarships are subject to federal income tax (even if they are spent on educational expenses).

**70. The answer is A.** Kamden and Octavia will receive a Child Tax Credit of $2,000 for their son, who is *under* the age of 17. Their daughter, who is age 17, does not qualify for the Child Tax Credit in 2023.

**71. The answer is C.** Rhett's gross income is calculated as follows:

| | |
|---|---|
| Wages reported on Form W-2 | $42,000 |
| Gambling winnings | $2,000 |
| Gambling losses | NO DEDUCTION |
| Dependent care benefits (spent $3,200 on childcare) | n/a |
| The deductible portion of capital loss carryover from the prior year | ($3,000) |
| **Gross income shown on the return** | **$41,000** |

The dependent care benefits are not taxable because Rhett's daycare expenses exceeded the benefit payments. The gross gambling winnings must be included in income. The gambling losses are only deductible as an itemized deduction and only to the extent of gambling winnings. If Rhett does not itemize his deductions, he cannot deduct his gambling losses. The capital loss carryover is deductible, but only up to $3,000, the annual capital loss deduction limit.

**72. The answer is B.** Royalties from copyrights, patents, oil, gas, and mineral properties are taxable as ordinary income. In most cases, royalties are reported as passive income on Schedule E. The amounts are generally subject to income tax, but *not* to self-employment tax. However, taxpayers who are in business as self-employed writers, inventors, artists, etc., must report this income on Schedule C, in which case the amounts would be subject to SE tax as well as income tax.

**73. The answer is B.** State income taxes are deductible on Schedule A. None of the other taxes are deductible. Taxpayers can only deduct up to a combined total of $10,000 ($5,000 if MFS) for state and local income, sales, and property taxes.

---

[26] IRS Notice 2014-7 addresses the income tax treatment of certain payments to an individual care provider under a state Home and Community-Based Services Waiver (Medicaid waiver) program. The notice provides that "qualified Medicaid waiver payments" as difficulty of care payments are excludable from gross income.

**74. The answer is D.** Abner and Viola are required to file a tax return, whether they file jointly or separately. Although Abner and Viola earned less than the standard deduction amount for married couples, a filing requirement is triggered because Abner received HSA distributions. Any taxpayer who received HSA, Archer MSA, or Medicare Advantage MSA distributions must file a return. Answer "C" is incorrect because if Abner were to file his own separate return (MFS), then Viola would be forced to file a separate return as well, because the filing threshold for MFS is only $5 of gross income in 2023.

**75. The answer is D.** The *refundable* additional child tax credit cannot be claimed by taxpayers who file Form 2555 and elect to exclude foreign-earned income from tax. The Child Tax Credit is claimed on Schedule 8812, *Credits for Qualifying Children and Other Dependents.*

**76. The answer is C.** Canceled debt is reported on Form 1099-C, *Cancellation of Debt.* It is not reported on Form 1099-MISC. Financial institutions and other creditors who forgive $600 or more are required to file Form 1099-C with the IRS as well as with the taxpayer.

**77. The answer is D.** A couple whose marriage was annulled cannot file jointly. Unlike divorce, an annulment legally invalidates a marriage and is effective on a *retroactive* basis. A court decree of annulment deems that no valid marriage ever existed. Therefore, the taxpayer is considered unmarried even if he or she filed joint returns for earlier years. A taxpayer whose marriage is annulled must file Form 1040-X, claiming single or HOH status for all tax years affected by the annulment that are not closed by the statute of limitations for filing an amended tax return.

**78. The answer is D.** Keenan cannot claim his stepdaughter as a dependent, because the child is not a U.S. citizen and not a resident of the United States, Canada, or Mexico. He may, however, file jointly with his nonresident alien spouse, providing that the spouses both agree to file together, and Seraphina requests an ITIN and elects to be treated as a U.S. resident for tax purposes. He can also choose to file MFS, and report only his own income on a separate return (question modified from an example in Publication 4491).

**79. The answer is B.** The amounts would be reported to Carla on 1099-MISC, not on Form W-2, because she did not earn the wages (her brother did). The income is considered IRD to Carla, and it is taxed as ordinary income, just as it would have been considered for the decedent, and Carla must report the income on her individual tax return. See Publication 559, *Survivors, Executors, and Administrators,* for a similar example.

**80. The answer is B.** Samuel can deduct a long-term capital loss of $500. Losses from the sale of property are disallowed between related parties. When the property is later sold to an *unrelated* party, any disallowed loss may be used to offset the *gain* on that transaction, but since Samuel sold the land at a loss, he cannot increase his deductible loss by the amount that was disallowed to his sister, Alexis.

**81. The answer is D.** Owen and Heloise must report the full amount **($22,000)** that was credited to their mutual fund account in 2023, regardless of the amount that was actually distributed to them. Capital gains distributions from a mutual fund are always reported as soon as they are *credited* to the taxpayer's mutual fund account, and they are also always treated as **long-term**, regardless of how long the taxpayer has held the shares. Investors may have to pay taxes on any capital gains distribution they receive, even if the fund performed poorly after they bought the shares.

**82. The answer is A.** Janet must report all of her income in 2023. She must recognize income in the year when she has constructive receipt of the funds. Constructive receipt occurred on December 26, 2023, when the check arrived at Janet's home and was available for Janet to deposit. It is not necessary for a taxpayer to have actual physical possession of the income. However, for constructive receipt to have taken place, funds must be available without substantial limitations. The fact that Janet was on vacation is irrelevant because the check was available for her to deposit.

**83. The answer is A.** Individuals, trusts, and estates with qualified business income may qualify for the 199A qualified business income (QBI) deduction. S corporations and partnerships cannot take the deduction themselves. However, all S corporations and partnerships report each shareholder's or partner's share of QBI on Schedule K-1, so each shareholder or partner may determine their QBI deduction on their individual Form 1040. The deduction is not available to C corporations or an employee that only earns wages.[27]

**84. The answer is B.** Isaiah is a *statutory employee.* Statutory employees are issued Forms W-2 by their employers, but they report their wages, income, and allowable expenses on Schedule C, just like self-employed taxpayers. The difference is that statutory employees are not required to pay self-employment tax, because their employers treat them as employees for Social Security tax purposes. Examples of statutory employees include:

- Full-time life insurance salespeople.
- Traveling salespeople.
- Certain commissioned truck drivers.
- Certain home workers who perform work on materials or goods furnished by the employer.

If a person is a statutory employee, the "statutory employee" box on Form W-2 should be checked.

---

[27] A notable exception to this rule exists for statutory employees. IRS Notice 2018-64 states that wages paid to statutory employees are qualifying income for the Section 199A deduction, in spite of the fact that the income is reported on Form W-2.

**85. The answer is C.** Leif's unemployment compensation is not qualifying income for purposes of an IRA contribution, and neither is his rental income. Since his wages were only $5,500 for the year, Leif has made a **$1,500 excess contribution** to his IRA. He must withdraw the excess contribution before the 2023 filing deadline, or he will have to pay an excise tax on any excess amount.

> **Note:** An excess IRA contribution, plus the earnings, will need to be removed by the filing deadline, including extensions. This is called a "corrective distribution," and it is done by notifying the IRA custodian, who will distribute the excess (along with any income earned on the excess). A special code on Form 1099-R will reflect that this is a corrective distribution.[28] If the overcontribution is not corrected, an excise tax will apply for every year the overcontribution remains in the account. The tax on excess contributions is 6%.

**86. The answer is B.** Brenda must list each payor and amount on Schedule B and file it with her individual tax return. Schedule B is required if any of the following applies:

- The taxpayer had over $1,500 of taxable interest or ordinary dividends.
- The taxpayer received interest from a seller-financed mortgage, and the buyer used the property as a personal residence.
- If a person has an interest in, or signature authority over, a foreign bank account (even if they have no interest or dividend income), they are also required to file a Schedule B to report the existence of the account.

**87. The answer is D.** Landry does not have to report any of his disability benefits. VA disability compensation is generally exempt from federal and state income tax, and from Social Security and Medicare taxes. The veteran must have been terminated through separation or discharge under honorable conditions. The VA does not issue Form W-2, Form 1099-R, or any other document for veterans' disability benefits.

**88. The answer is A.** Minnie does not qualify for the Educator Expense Deduction (previously called the "Teacher Credit") because she has only 440 hours of documented employment as an educator during the tax year. She cannot deduct her educator expenses because she is not a qualified educator for the purposes of the deduction. An "eligible educator" is a K-12 teacher, instructor, counselor, principal or aide that works at least 900 hours a year in a school that provides elementary or secondary education.

**89. The answer is A.** Kristine cannot deduct the value of her time as a charitable contribution. The value of a person's time and service is not deductible as a charitable expense. All of the other donations are allowed as a charitable deduction.

---

[28] If a retirement plan makes a corrective distribution of excess amounts (excess deferrals or excess contributions), the taxpayer's Form 1099-R should have the code "8" or "P" in box 7 (code "B" if from a ROTH IRA).

**90. The answer is D.** Calder's gross profit is **$25,000** ($125,000 selling price - $100,000 adjusted basis), and his gross profit percentage is 20% ($25,000 ÷ $125,000). He must report 20% of each payment received (excluding the portion representing interest income) as gain from the sale. Thus, **$5,000** (20% of the $25,000 down payment) is taxable in the current year. An "installment sale" is a sale of property where the seller receives at least one payment after the tax year in which the sale occurs. The most common type of installment sale is the sale of real estate. Installment sale rules only apply when there is a profit on the sale; they don't apply to sales that result in a loss (this question is modified from an example in Publication 537, *Installment Sales*).

**91. The answer is B.** Emmett's compensatory damages resulting from personal physical injuries or physical sickness, including reimbursement of medical bills (that were not previously deducted) and lost wages, are generally not taxable income, whether they are from a settlement or from an actual court award, (unless they are specifically described as punitive damages). However, any interest associated with an award or settlement is always taxable, so he must report the $15,000 in interest.

**92. The answer is A.** Clarita would likely qualify for the Child and Dependent Care Credit, since she pays for a caregiver for her disabled mother, who is her dependent and a "qualifying person" for the credit. The credit does not only apply to daycare expenses for children. A "qualifying individual" for the purposes of the Child and Dependent Care Credit includes:

- A child under the age of 13, or
- A spouse or other dependent who was physically or mentally disabled.

Answer "B" is incorrect because Clarita's gross income exceeds the limits for the EITC for her filing status. Answer "C" is incorrect because Clarita had job-based health insurance all year, and the Advanced Premium Tax Credit only applies to taxpayers who obtain their health insurance from the Healthcare Marketplace. Answer "D" is incorrect because Clarita doesn't have a dependent child (only a dependent parent), so she would not qualify for the Child Tax Credit.

**93. The answer is C.** Morgaine is subject to the Kiddie Tax. Morgaine's *unearned* income totals $4,300. This is the total of her dividends ($3,300), taxable interest ($900), and capital gains reduced by her capital losses ($500 - $400 = $100). Her wages are considered *earned* income rather than unearned income because they are for work performed, so the wages are not included in the calculation. Her tax-exempt interest is also not considered in determining unearned income for this purpose.

> **Note:** The kiddie tax only applies to unearned income in excess of $2,500 in 2023. Regular tax rates apply to the amounts under this threshold, which is exempt from the kiddie tax. The remaining unearned income is subject to the kiddie tax and will be taxed at her *parents'* marginal tax rate.

**94. The answer is A.** Rowan does not have to report the gain on the sale because it qualifies for exclusion under Section 121. Rowan would normally not meet the "use test" in the five-year period before the sale. However, Rowan is subject to special rules for military personnel because he was on qualified official extended duty. In general, to qualify for the Section 121 exclusion, a taxpayer must meet both the ownership test and the use test, which means that the taxpayer must have "owned and used" the home as a primary residence at least two years out of the five years prior to its date of sale. However, a taxpayer on qualified official extended duty in the U.S. Armed Forces may elect to suspend the five-year test period for up to ten years.

**95. The answer is B.** Tobias can claim head of household status since his wife is a nonresident alien who will not file a joint return with him, and he meets all the other qualifications for head of household. There is a special exception that allows U.S. citizens and U.S. resident aliens who live with their *nonresident* alien spouses to file as head of household. In order to qualify for this exception, all of the following requirements must be met:

- The taxpayer is a U.S. citizen or resident alien for the entire year and meets all the rules for head of household *except for* living with the nonresident alien spouse.
- The nonresident alien spouse does not meet the substantial presence test.
- The nonresident alien spouse does not choose to file a joint return with the taxpayer.

**96. The answer is A.** Passive activity losses are generally deductible only to the extent of passive activity income. Passive activity income can only be generated by a passive activity. There are only two sources of passive activity income:

1. A passive rental activity, or
2. A business activity in which the taxpayer does not materially participate.

Nonpassive activities are businesses in which the taxpayer works on a regular, continuous, and substantial basis. In addition, passive activity income does NOT include salaries, portfolio income, or investment income. As a general rule, the passive activity loss rules are applied at the individual level. Income and losses from the following activities would generally be treated as passive activities:

- Rental real estate (exceptions exist for real estate professionals).
- Farming activity in which the taxpayer does not materially participate.
- Limited partnerships with some exceptions.
- Partnerships, S-Corporations, and limited liability companies in which the taxpayer does not *materially participate* in the activity.

There are two exceptions to this passive activity loss limitation. First, when a taxpayer materially participates in a business, it is not generally considered a passive activity. Second, although rental real estate income is generally considered passive activity income, there is an exception in the law for real estate professionals.

**97. The answer is B.** The maximum taxable amount of a taxpayer's Social Security benefits subject to tax is 85%, regardless of their AGI. Roseanne has enough additional income, based on her filing status, to have the maximum amount of Social Security benefits subject to tax. Therefore, the maximum amount that is taxable on Roseanne's net benefits is 85% or **$10,540** ($12,400 × .85).

**98. The answer is C.** The FBAR is filed with the FinCEN (the Financial Crimes Enforcement Network), and Form 8938 is filed with the IRS. The Form 8938 is filed along with a taxpayer's individual tax return, while the FBAR is submitted as a separate filing directly on the FinCEN's website.

**99. The answer is A.** Roth IRAs offer tax-free growth and tax-free withdrawals in retirement. Roth IRA contributions are always made with after-tax dollars. Unlike traditional IRAs, Roth IRAs do not require RMDs. Withdrawals from a Roth IRA are not required until after the death of the IRA owner.

**100. The answer is A.** Sawyer's taxable estate is calculated as follows:

| | |
|---|---|
| Cash and investments | $6,325,000 |
| Life insurance proceeds payable to beneficiaries | 10,000,000 |
| Personal residence (his one-half share) | 250,000 |
| Subtotal – gross estate | **16,575,000** |
| Funeral expenses | (25,000) |
| Legal/Administration expenses | (50,000) |
| Debts outstanding at the time of death | (200,000) |
| Estate value before marital deduction | 16,300,000 |
| Marital deduction | (16,300,000) |
| **Taxable estate** | **$0** |

Because Sawyer's spouse is a U.S. citizen, his estate is entitled to an unlimited marital deduction for assets passing to his spouse (up to the amount of his taxable estate). An estate tax return must be filed (Form 706) because the value of the estate is above the exemption threshold, but no estate tax will be due.

# #3 Sample Exam: Individuals

**(Please test yourself first; then check the correct answers at the end of this exam.)**

1. Harold lost his job in 2023, and had financial difficulties paying his home mortgage. He contacted his lender and negotiated a workout agreement on October 1, 2023, thereby reducing the amount he owed on the mortgage and staying in the home. Harold's lender agreed to reduce his mortgage debt from $195,000 to $175,000. The lender issued a Form 1099-C showing $20,000 of canceled debt. Harold was not insolvent or in bankruptcy at the time of the cancellation, and the mortgage is a recourse loan. Is this amount taxable to Harold, and if so, how should it be reported on his tax return?

| | | | |
|---|---|---|---|
| | ☐ CORRECTED (if checked) | | |
| CREDITOR'S name, street address, city or town, state or province, country, ZIP or foreign postal code, and telephone no.<br><br>HOME MORTGAGE LOAN<br>1111 ANYWHERE STREET<br>ANYWHERE TOWN, STATE ZIP | **1** Date of identifiable event<br>**10-1-2023** | OMB No. 1545-1424<br>Form **1099-C**<br>(Rev. January 2022) | **Cancellation of Debt** |
| | **2** Amount of debt discharged<br>$ **$20,000** | | |
| | **3** Interest, if included in box 2<br>$ | For calendar year<br>20 **23** | |
| CREDITOR'S TIN<br>**11-1111111** | DEBTOR'S TIN<br>**123-45-6789** | **4** Debt description<br><br>HOME MORTGAGE LOAN<br>1111 ANYWHERE STREET<br>ANYWHERE TOWN, STATE ZIP | **Copy B**<br>**For Debtor**<br>This is important tax information and is being furnished to the IRS. If you are required to file a return, a negligence penalty or other sanction may be imposed on you if taxable income results from this transaction and the IRS determines that it has not been reported. |
| DEBTOR'S name<br>**HAROLD SMITH** | | | |
| Street address (including apt. no.)<br>**123 MAIN ST** | | **5** If checked, the debtor was personally liable for repayment of the debt . . . . . . . . .  **X** | |
| City or town, state or province, country, and ZIP or foreign postal code<br>**ANYTOWN, TX 80000** | | | |
| Account number (see instructions) | | **6** Identifiable event code | **7** Fair market value of property<br>$ |

Form **1099-C** (Rev. 1-2022)   (keep for your records)   www.irs.gov/Form1099C   Department of the Treasury - Internal Revenue Service

A. The $20,000 in canceled debt is not taxable and does not have to be reported on his return.

B. The $20,000 in canceled debt is not taxable, but must be reported on Form 982.

C. The $20,000 in canceled debt is taxable and needs to be reported on Schedule D.

D. The $20,000 in canceled debt is taxable and needs to be reported on Schedule D and Form 8949.

2. Jiro is unmarried. He died on July 1, 2023. At the time of his death, he owned several rental properties that continued to earn revenue after he died. How should the income from the rental properties be reported *after* the date of his death?

A. All the rental income should be reported on his final Form 1040.

B. The rental income received after Jiro's death should be reported on Form 1041.

C. The rental income earned after his death should be reported on the beneficiary's tax return.

D. The income from the rentals should be reported on Form 706.

3. Personal home mortgage interest is only deductible on Schedule A if the mortgage loan is:

A. Secured by the home.
B. Less than $750,000.
C. On a primary residence.
D. Based on a taxpayer's gross income.

4. On February 22, 2023, Roland was awarded $159,000 for compensatory damages due to physical injury from a serious auto accident. Roland was also awarded $625,000 in punitive damages from the same lawsuit. He paid $55,000 in legal fees during the year. He had no other income or expenses during the year. What is Roland's reportable gross income for the year?

A. $0
B. $570,000
C. $625,000
D. $784,000

5. Aurora and Crispin are married and file jointly. Crispin's salary is $180,000, and Aurora's wages are $150,000. They have no other income or adjustments for the year. Their total combined income is $330,000 ($180,000 + $150,000). What is the amount of their *Additional Medicare Tax* (the threshold for MFJ is $250,000)?

A. $450
B. $720
C. $1,200
D. $2,400

6. Personal, non-business tax preparation fees are deductible as:

A. A miscellaneous itemized deduction subject to the 2% limit.
B. An investment expense on Schedule A.
C. An investment expense on Form 4592.
D. Tax preparation fees are generally not deductible.

7. Which of the following personal casualty and theft losses would be deductible as an itemized deduction on Schedule A?

A. Theft of personal jewelry.
B. Destruction of a personal-use vehicle in an auto accident.
C. Flood damage to a main home in a federal disaster area.
D. Decline in home value due to graffiti.

8. Tammy is 27 years old and unmarried. She is also legally blind. In 2023, Tammy has interest income of $1,900 from an investment that she inherited from her grandfather. She also earned wages of $12,900. She does not plan to itemize. What is her standard deduction amount?

A. $4,400
B. $12,950
C. $14,800
D. $15,700

9. Jason is 52 and unmarried. He has an AGI of $62,000 in 2023. Jason's two daughters, Ginger and Taylor, lived with him the entire year. Ginger is 23 and a full-time college student, studying for her first bachelor's degree. Taylor is 16 and a full-time high-school student. Both children have valid social security numbers. Jason provides all the financial support for his two daughters. He also provided all the costs of keeping up the home for the year. Can Jason claim the Child Tax Credit (CTC) or the Credit for Other Dependents (ODC) for his daughters?

A. Both daughters are qualifying children for the Credit for Other Dependents.
B. Both daughters are qualifying children for the Child Tax Credit.
C. Taylor qualifies for the Child Tax Credit, and Ginger qualifies for the Credit for Other Dependents.
D. Neither Ginger nor Taylor are qualifying children for either credit.

10. Enrique and Anita divorced six years ago. They have one child together, Juana, who lives with Anita. All are U.S. citizens and have valid Social Security numbers that are valid for employment. Anita's AGI is $29,000. Enrique's AGI is $59,000. Juana is 13 years old and has no income. Juana stays with her father two days a week. Although Anita is the custodial parent, Anita signed Form 8332 to give the dependency exemption to Enrique. Which of the following statements is correct?

A. Enrique can claim his daughter Juana as a dependent and claim the Earned Income Credit.
B. Enrique can claim his daughter Juana as a dependent and also claim the Child Tax Credit.
C. Neither Enrique nor Anita can claim Juana as a dependent or any of the other benefits.
D. Only Anita can claim her daughter Juana as a dependent since she is the custodial parent.

11. Which of the following is NOT a requirement for a foreign tax to be considered creditable and thus allowable to be used to compute the Foreign Tax Credit?

A. The tax must be imposed on the taxpayer.
B. The taxpayer must have paid or accrued the tax.
C. The tax must be incurred while the taxpayer has a foreign tax home.
D. The tax must be the legal and actual foreign tax liability.

12. Five years ago, Penelope's employer, the Burnside Corporation, offered Penelope 100 shares of restricted stock at a discounted price of $10 a share. At the time of the sale, the fair market value of the stock was $100 a share. Under the terms of the sale, the stock is not vested until Penelope completes a mandatory 5-year employment period (if she does not stay the required 5-year period, she must forfeit the stock). In 2023, at the end of the 5-year period, the stock is fully vested, and the fair market value of the stock has increased to $200 a share. How much income would Penelope report in 2023?

A. $0
B. $1,000
C. $10,000
D. $19,000

13. Thor, age 46, is single and covered by a retirement plan at work. He has maxed out his contributions to his 401(k) plan at work. His AGI in 2023 is $179,000. Can Thor *also* contribute to a traditional IRA?

A. He can make a $7,500 deductible contribution to his traditional IRA.
B. He can make a $6,500 non-deductible contribution to his traditional IRA.
C. He is not allowed to make a contribution to a traditional IRA because he is covered by a retirement plan at work and has already contributed to his 401(k).
D. He cannot contribute to a traditional IRA, but he can contribute to a Roth IRA.

14. Kirby bought his home on May 30, 2018. He originally purchased the home for $220,000. After he lost his job, he was not able to make the mortgage payments. The bank foreclosed on the home on January 10, 2023, and Kirby moved out. On the date of the foreclosure, the fair market value of the home had dropped to $185,000 because of flood damage that had occurred the year before. The principal balance of the mortgage, which happened to be a recourse debt in the state he lives in, was $195,000. All of the debt was incurred to purchase the home. Kirby received Form 1099-C for the amount of debt canceled by his bank. Is this a taxable event, and how should he report this on his tax return?

A. The cancellation of debt is not taxable. He should file Form 8949 and Schedule D to report the disposition of the home and Form 982 to exclude the debt cancellation.
B. The cancellation of debt is taxable. He should file Form 8949 and Schedule D to report the disposition of the home.
C. The cancellation of debt is not taxable. He only needs to file Form 982 to exclude the debt cancellation.
D. Since the mortgage is recourse debt, the cancellation of debt is taxable. Kirby should file Schedule D to report the disposition of the home.

15. Which of the following is NOT a requirement for a taxpayer to claim the foreign earned income exclusion (FEIE)?

A. Have foreign earned income.
B. Have a tax home in a foreign country.
C. Meet either the bona fide residence or the physical presence test.
D. Be a United States citizen.

16. Camilla is a self-employed accountant. She took her best client to a hockey game. The event was sold out, so Camilla paid $200 for both tickets through a ticket scalper, which was almost double the $60 face value of each ticket. After the game, Camilla and her client went to dinner at a local restaurant and discussed business. The total meal cost was $80, and the taxi ride to the restaurant cost $20. Based on this information, how much can Camilla deduct as a business expense?

A. $0
B. $60
C. $80
D. $300

17. Which of the following forms is used to report gambling income to a taxpayer?

A. Form 1099-G
B. Form 1099-NEC
C. Form W-2G
D. Form W-2

18. Jennifer and Colton adopted twin boys from China during the year. The adoption was final on December 10, 2023. They incurred the following fees related to the adoption.

- $20,000 in legal fees,
- $15,000 in travel expenses
- $13,000 in adoption agency fees

Their joint AGI is $210,000. What is the maximum adoption credit that they can claim on their 2023 tax return?

A. $0
B. $15,950
C. $31,900
D. $48,000

19. Murray is an elementary school teacher who works full-time in a private Christian school. He had 1,900 hours of documented employment during the tax year. Murray spent $295 on school supplies for his students. Of that amount, $220 was for educational software. The other $95 was for supplies for a course he teaches on reproductive health. What expenses can he deduct as an adjustment to income?

A. $220
B. $295
C. $300
D. $315

20. Abram and Dawn file a joint return. They are both U.S. citizens, and they have valid SSNs. Their tax liability is $2,000. They have three dependents that lived in their household all year. None of the dependents earned any taxable income during the year.

1.   Abel is their 21-year-old son and has an SSN. He is not a student or disabled.
2.   Imelda is their 16-year-old niece, and she has an ITIN.
3.   Martina is Abram's mother. She is 75 years old, has a valid SSN and meets the qualifying relative test.

Imelda, Abel, and Martina are all U.S. residents for tax purposes. Which of them is a qualifying dependent for the Credit for Other Dependents?

A. Abel, Imelda, and Martina.
B. Abel and Martina only.
C. Abel only.
D. Martina only.

21. Beckett is a self-employed paralegal. Beckett attends a legal conference in Los Angeles, CA, on July 10, 2023. His expenses related to the trip were as follows:

| | |
|---|---|
| Hotel lodging | $300 |
| Airfare to the event | $245 |
| Meals | $40 |
| Registration fees for the legal conference | $450 |
| A golf outing with a vendor the following day (business was discussed) | $230 |

What amount is Beckett's deductible business expense for the trip on his Schedule C?

A. $885
B. $1,015
C. $1,035
D. $1,245

22. Arlene is single and has a regular full-time job as a bank manager. She also trades digital assets (cryptocurrency) as a casual investor. She is not a professional securities broker and only trades digital assets as an investment. Her cryptocurrency exchange does not issue an information statement to her at the end of the year. How should Arlene report the income she received selling virtual currency?

A. "Other income" on Form 1040.
B. Schedule D and Schedule B.
C. Schedule D and Form 8949.
D. Schedule D only.

23. Holton is single and age 49. On January 13, 2023, he withdrew $30,000 from his traditional IRA to pay off some credit card debt, but changed his mind almost immediately and redeposited the entire sum back into a different traditional IRA account on February 13, 2023. Will he be subject to a penalty?

A. He will have to pay a 10% penalty on the amount withdrawn.
B. He has made an excess contribution to his IRA, and he will be subject to a 6% excise tax.
C. He will pay income tax and penalties on the amount in excess of $6,500.
D. He will not have to pay a penalty because he returned the money to the IRA within 60 days.

24. Benito, age 36, made a $6,500 contribution to his traditional IRA on February 1, 2023. He forgot that he had made the contribution, and on December 26, 2023, he deposited another $6,500 into a Roth IRA account. What is the consequence of these transactions?

A. Benito has made an excess contribution of $6,500. He must withdraw the excess contribution from either one of his IRA accounts by the filing deadline or face a penalty.
B. The second contribution is a prohibited transaction. His Roth IRA is disqualified and he must pay tax on the entire balance in the account.
C. As long as he designates his traditional IRA contribution as nondeductible, he can leave both contributions in his IRA accounts.
D. There are no tax consequences since Benito deposited the funds into different types of IRA accounts (a traditional IRA and a Roth IRA).

25. What is the Premium Tax Credit?

A. A credit based on a qualifying child.
B. A credit for higher education.
C. A credit for employers who offer health insurance to their employees.
D. A credit to make health insurance premiums more affordable.

26. Samuel works as an independent contractor for Herder Construction Company. He does private safety consulting. Herder Construction Company sent Samuel a Form 1099-NEC that shows he received $12,500 for the work he did for them. He also received cash payments of $6,200 from several different individuals for private jobs that he completed. He did not receive Forms 1099-NEC for this additional $6,200. Which of the following is true?

A. The $12,500 is taxable income and should be reported on Schedule C. The other income is not taxable because Samuel did not get a Form 1099-NEC for it.
B. Samuel must include the $6,200 in cash payments as self-employment income along with the $12,500 on Form 1099-NEC. All the income should be reported on Schedule C.
C. Samuel must report all the income on Form 1040 as regular wages.
D. Samuel must include the $6,200 in cash payments as self-employment income along with the $12,500 on Form 1099-NEC. The 1099 income should be reported on Schedule C. The other $6,200 in income should be reported as "Other Income" on Form 1040.

27. Waverly is a self-employed veterinarian. She is unmarried and does not have any dependents. She has $275,500 of net income on Schedule C. Waverly paid $14,000 in self-employed health insurance premiums during the year, and her total self-employment tax was $24,784. Her modified taxable income was $235,258. Her only income is from her business, which is a Specified Service Trade or Business (SSTB). What is the amount of her section 199A qualified business deduction in 2023?

A. $0
B. $49,721
C. $52,200
D. $55,000

28. Sampson is single and 73 years old. He works full-time, and he earns $179,000 in wages during the year. He is not covered by a workplace retirement plan, so he wants to make a contribution to an IRA. What is the maximum amount that he can contribute to an IRA in 2023?

A. He cannot contribute to an IRA because he is over age 70½.
B. He can contribute a maximum of $7,500 to a Roth IRA.
C. He can contribute a maximum of $6,500 to a traditional IRA or a Roth IRA.
D. He can contribute a maximum of $7,500 to a traditional IRA.

29. In 2023, for purposes of the Child Tax Credit, a "qualifying child" is a child who:

A. Is under the age of 18 (or disabled of any age).
B. Is under the age of 17 and claimed as a dependent on the taxpayer's return.
C. Lived with the taxpayer for the entire year, regardless of age.
D. Is either under the age of 19 or a full-time student under the age of 24.

30. Carly is unmarried. She dies on March 27, 2023. She earned $24,000 in wages before her death, and her executor is required to file a final return for her. At the time of her death, Carly had $40,000 in outstanding student loans. The loan was later discharged, and Carly's executor received a 1099-C showing $40,000 in canceled student loan debt. Carly was not insolvent or in bankruptcy at the time of her death. What is the proper treatment of this canceled debt on Carly's final Form 1040?

A. The canceled debt is not taxable.
B. The canceled debt is fully taxable.
C. The canceled debt is only partially taxable, up to the amount of her taxable income.
D. The canceled debt is taxable to Carly's estate.

31. Interest received on a municipal bond is generally:

A. Fully taxable.
B. Partially taxable.
C. Tax-exempt.
D. Taxable when earned.

32. On July 1, 2023, Heidi received a condo as a gift from her mother, Serena. Her mother had owned and lived in the condo for a decade, and the property was completely paid off. On the date of the gift, the condo had a fair market value of $94,000 and an original cost basis of $60,000. Heidi didn't use the condo as a residence, and she ends up selling it quickly for $91,000 on November 20, 2023. What is the amount and character of her gain (or loss) on this transaction?

A. Heidi has a short-term capital loss of $3,000.
B. Heidi has a long-term capital gain of $31,000.
C. Heidi has a short-term capital gain of $31,000.
D. Heidi has a short-term capital gain of $34,000.

33. Vienna is single and just finished her accounting degree. She takes a full-time job at an accounting firm on June 10, 2023, and immediately starts paying down her student loans. She earns $69,000 in wages during the year and pays $3,800 in student loan interest. She has no other income or losses for the year. How much of Vienna's student loan interest is deductible in 2023?

A. $0.
B. $2,000
C. $2,500
D. $3,800

34. Broderick is a U.S. Airman serving overseas in Europe. He received several items of income during the year related to his military duty. Which of the following types of income would *not* be taxable to Broderick?

A. Qualified hazardous duty pay.
B. A reenlistment bonus.
C. Pay for accrued leave.
D. Differential wage payments.

35. Kenny and Glynda own a home in Los Angeles, CA, which they have always used as their primary residence. They purchased the house on January 19, 2021, for $295,000. They sold it on December 29, 2023, for $329,000. At the time of the sale, they had an existing mortgage on the property of $180,000. They use the sales proceeds to purchase a new home in Florida for $375,000. Their only other income for the year was $28,000 in Social Security income. They will file jointly. What is the amount of their taxable gain on this transaction?

A. $0
B. $34,000
C. $115,000
D. $329,000

36. Rebecca works as a real estate agent for Beemer Realty Services. She visits the company's real estate offices at least once a day to check her mail. She manages dozens of listings and splits her real estate commissions with Beemer Realty, her sole source of income. How should Rebecca be classified by Beemer Realty?

A. Employee.
B. Statutory employee.
C. Corporate shareholder.
D. Statutory nonemployee.

37. Which of the following statements is correct regarding Form 1095-A, *Health Insurance Marketplace Statement?*

A. Taxpayers do not need Form 1095-A to complete Form 8962, Premium Tax Credit, to reconcile advance payments of the premium tax credit or claim the premium tax credit on their tax return.
B. Taxpayers will receive Form 1095-A if they have been covered by an employer insurance plan.
C. Taxpayers must use Form 1095-A to complete Form 8962, Premium Tax Credit, to reconcile advance payments of the premium tax credit or claim the premium tax credit on their tax return.
D. Taxpayers who purchase insurance from the Marketplace must attach Form 1095-A to their individual tax return to prove their insurance coverage.

38. Debbie wants to file her 2023 tax return. However, on March 3, 2024, she still had not received her Form W-2 from her employer. What is the *first* thing she should do?

A. Contact the Taxpayer Advocate for assistance.
B. File her tax return using her last paystub.
C. File her tax return without Form W-2 using Form 4852, Substitute W-2.
D. Contact her employer to get the Form W-2.

39. Ximena is 26 and single. She received a Form W-2 for $14,000 in wages from her part-time job. She also received a $4,000 college scholarship. However, she dropped out of college three days before the Spring semester began. She did not attend any classes in 2023. She used the $4,000 in scholarship funds to buy a used car instead. What is the correct treatment of these income amounts?

A. Ximena's wages are taxable, but the scholarship is not.
B. Ximena does not have to file a return because her income is below the filing requirement.
C. Ximena should report only her wage income and write "EXEMPT" next to the scholarship amount on Schedule 1, Form 1040.
D. Ximena must report both the wages and the scholarship as taxable income. She would report the taxable scholarship amount on line 8r of Schedule 1 (Form 1040).

40. Which of the following types of debt cancellation must be reported as taxable income?

A. $35,000 of credit card debt canceled in a Title 11 bankruptcy case.
B. $50,000 of canceled mortgage debt on a vacation home for a solvent taxpayer.
C. $65,000 of canceled credit card debt for an insolvent taxpayer (the taxpayer is insolvent by $97,000).
D. $90,000 of canceled debt on a primary residence.

41. Which of the following miscellaneous itemized deductions are still allowable in 2023?

A. Safety deposit box rental.
B. Tax preparation fees.
C. Union dues.
D. Impairment-related work expenses of a disabled employee.

42. Which of the following income may be subject to the Net Investment Income Tax (NIIT)?

A. Notary fees.
B. Taxable mutual fund distributions.
C. Tax-exempt municipal bond interest.
D. Traditional IRA distributions.

43. Frank owns several types of investment and custodial accounts. Frank files as Head of Household and claims his 12-year-old daughter, Marybeth, on his tax return. Frank has an AGI of $46,000 from wages and a high-deductible health plan (HDHP). Which of the following contributions would *not* be tax-deductible?

A. A $4,000 contribution to a traditional IRA account.
B. A $2,000 contribution to his daughter's Coverdell ESA.
C. A $1,600 contribution to his Health Savings Account.
D. All of the above contributions are deductible.

44. For IRS purposes, how many months does a child have to be enrolled in school in order to be considered a "full-time student"?

A. A full-time student for IRS purposes is one enrolled for some part of five calendar months.
B. The student must have over six months of full-time enrollment.
C. The student must be enrolled for at least nine months.
D. The student must have twelve consecutive months of full-time enrollment.

45. Sebastian, age 61, and Ruby, age 49, are married and file jointly. They both want to contribute to their retirement accounts this year. Sebastian has $69,000 in wages. Ruby has only $2,000 in wages from a part-time job. Based on this information, what is the maximum that they can contribute to their individual retirement accounts in 2023?

A. They can each contribute $6,500.
B. They can each contribute $7,500.
C. Sebastian can contribute $6,500, and Ruby can contribute $2,000.
D. Sebastian can contribute $7,500, and Ruby can contribute $6,500.

46. On March 3, 2023, Kenneth, age 42, was involved in a serious automobile accident, leaving him permanently disabled. On August 10, 2023, Kenneth withdrew $24,000 from his traditional IRA account. He provided proof of his permanent disability to his IRA trustee when he made the withdrawal. What are the consequences of this distribution?

A. The IRA withdrawal will be subject to income tax and a 10% early withdrawal penalty because Kenneth is not 59½ years of age.
B. The IRA withdrawal will be subject to income tax and a 25% early withdrawal penalty because Kenneth is not 59½ years of age.
C. The IRA withdrawal will be subject to income tax but will not be subject to an early withdrawal penalty because Kenneth is permanently disabled.
D. The IRA withdrawal will not be subject to income tax or an early withdrawal penalty because Kenneth is permanently disabled.

47. Dharma incurs the following medical expenses during the year. She earns $40,500 in wages and has no other income for the year. What is the total amount of her qualified medical expenses before the application of any income limitations?

| Medical expenses | Amount |
|---|---|
| Teeth Whitening | $500 |
| Prescription medicines shipped from other countries | $1,200 |
| Insulin | $300 |
| Health Club Dues | $500 |
| Life insurance premiums | $400 |
| Vision correction surgery (LASIK) | $6,700 |
| Dental insurance premiums | $2,000 |
| Smoking-cessation program (prescribed by a doctor) | $450 |

A. $9,000
B. $9,450
C. $10,200
D. $10,650

48. Jasper is a U.S. citizen who lives and works in South America. He works online and does not remain in any one country for more than 60 days. Instead, he travels around a lot and visits multiple foreign nations throughout the year. In order for him to qualify for the Foreign Earned Income Exclusion, he must be physically present in a foreign country (or multiple foreign countries) for at least _____ full days during a period of 12 consecutive months.

A. 180
B. 246
C. 330
D. 365

49. The requirement to file the FinCEN Form 114 (FBAR) is triggered if a U.S. person has a financial interest or signature authority over any foreign financial account, but only if the aggregate value of these accounts exceeds ____ anytime during the year.

A. $10,000
B. $50,000
C. $75,000
D. $100,000

50. Which of the following types of income would be reported on Form 1099-MISC?

A. Nonemployee compensation.
B. Canceled debt income.
C. Interest income.
D. Crop insurance proceeds of $600 or more.

51. In 2023, which of the following types of interest is not deductible on Schedule A?

A. Investment interest for loans used to purchase taxable investments.
B. Mortgage interest on a primary residence.
C. Home equity loan interest incurred to buy a personal car.
D. Mortgage interest incurred on a vacation home.

52. In 2008, Ashton and Moana claimed the $7,500 First-Time Homebuyer Credit. The couple has used their home as a primary residence since then. In 2023, they converted the home into a rental property. What, if any, is their tax obligation regarding the First-Time Homebuyer Credit?

A. Ashton and Moana must pay the entire unpaid balance of the credit.
B. They must pro-rate the credit received over 15 years and repay 50% of the original credit.
C. They must reduce their depreciable basis in the property by the unpaid balance of the credit.
D. Since they used this home as a primary residence for two of the last five years, there is no requirement to repay.

53. Egbert is 71 and married but files separately from his wife. He has lived apart from his spouse for the entire year. What is Egbert's "base amount" for computing the taxable portion of his Social Security benefits?

A. $0
B. $10,000
C. $25,000
D. $32,000

54. Pearl is 65 and a self-employed loan-signing agent and notary. She had $12,000 in Social Security income during the year, as well as other types of income from various sources. In order to calculate if her Social Security benefits are taxable, all of the following are included *except*:

A. Tax-exempt muni bond interest.
B. Life insurance proceeds.
C. Notary fees received.
D. Self-employment income.

55. Courtney is employed full-time as a nurse. She is 35 and files MFS. She had been separated from her spouse for three years, but has not filed for divorce or legal separation. Her AGI for 2023 was $48,200. Of this amount, $3,000 was from gambling winnings. She had the following itemized deductions in 2023:

| | |
|---|---|
| Mortgage interest paid on a main home | $6,700 |
| Property tax on a main home | $5,300 |
| Employee-related business expenses | $5,200 |
| Charitable donation to a church | $2,600 |
| Gambling losses | $6,600 |

What amount is deductible on her Schedule A?

A. $11,136
B. $17,300
C. $17,600
D. $26,400

56. Which of the following retirement plans offer a tax deduction on contributions?

A. Traditional IRA
B. Roth IRA
C. Roth 401(k)
D. Coverdell ESA

57. Jada is unmarried and lives in San Diego, CA. In 2023, Jada earned $45,000 in wages and sold her principal residence for $1 million. She has owned and lived in the home continuously for the last ten years. Jada's cost basis in the home is $600,000, so her realized gain on the sale is $400,000. She is eligible for the Section 121 exclusion, so the amount subject to income taxes is $150,000 ($400,000 realized gain less the $250,000 exclusion). She has no other gain or loss during the year. What is Jada's modified adjusted gross income (MAGI), and how much of her income is subject to the Net Investment Income Tax (the threshold amount is $200,000 for single filers)?

A. Jada's modified adjusted gross income is $195,000. None of her income is subject to the Net Investment Income Tax.
B. Jada's modified adjusted gross income is $445,000. And $150,000 is subject to the Net Investment Income Tax.
C. Jada's modified adjusted gross income is $195,000. And $150,000 of her income is subject to the Net Investment Income Tax.
D. Jada's modified adjusted gross income is $195,000. And $45,000 of her income is subject to the Net Investment Income Tax.

58. Bertrand is a U.S. citizen who lives and works overseas in Austria. His wife, Eliana, is a nonresident alien and a citizen of Austria. Bertrand and Eliana file a joint return, to which they attach a statement declaring an election to treat Eliana as a U.S. resident for tax purposes. Which of the following events would end the election in a later year?

A. Bertrand becomes self-employed.
B. Bertrand dies.
C. Bertrand and Eliana fail to attach a statement to their tax return in future years.
D. Bertrand and Eliana file separate returns the next year.

59. Which of the following is not an AMT "preference item" for determining the Alternative Minimum Tax for individuals?

A. Capital gains from the exercise of stock options.
B. The qualifying exclusion for small business stock.
C. Interest from muni bonds exempt from regular tax.
D. Qualified charitable contributions.

60. Ursula owns several investments. During the year, she receives a Form-1099-DIV showing $3,200 in ordinary dividends. How will these dividends be taxed on her individual tax return?

A. Reported on Schedule B as long-term capital gains.
B. Reported on Schedule B as ordinary income.
C. Reported on Schedule D as a long-term capital gain.
D. Reported on Schedule D as ordinary income.

61. Which form is used by individual taxpayers to change their income tax withholding with their employer?

A. Form W-4
B. Form W-7
C. Form W-2
D. Form I-9

62. Everly is single. She plans to itemize her deductions. Which of the following expenses would *not* be deductible on Schedule A?

A. A personal casualty loss on her home that occurred in a federally declared disaster area.
B. Qualified medical expenses that were paid with a distribution from her HSA.
C. A charitable contribution to a veteran's organization.
D. Sales tax on the purchase of a vehicle.

63. Lynne is employed as a part-time secretary for a clothing manufacturer. On July 1, 2023, Lynne quits her job and moves to another state for a new job. She has the following mileage expenses in 2023:

| Type of Mileage | Miles |
|---|---|
| Mileage while volunteering at various charities | 700 |
| Unreimbursed mileage incurred running errands for her employer | 125 |
| Commuting mileage from her home to her regular workplace | 2,900 |
| Mileage incurred while moving due to a new job (over 50 miles away) | 1,200 |

Ignoring any AGI limitations, what dollar amount would be deductible on her Schedule A as an itemized deduction?

A. $0
B. $98
C. $476
D. $544

64. Della is 23 and divorced. She and her 4-year-old daughter, Geraldine, lived with Della's father, Layton, all year. Layton paid all the costs of keeping up the home. Della provides the majority of her own support, but Layton helps support Geraldine, his granddaughter. Della's AGI is $19,000. Layton's AGI is $45,000. Based on these facts, which of the following statements is correct?

A. Della can file as Head of Household, claim her daughter as a dependent and claim the EITC.
B. Della can file as Head of Household and claim her daughter as a dependent, but she can't claim EITC.
C. Della can file as single, claim her daughter as a dependent, and claim the EITC.
D. Della cannot claim her daughter as a dependent.

65. Irene owns a residential rental property in Montana with an adjusted basis of $17,000 and a fair market value of $40,000. During the year, she trades her existing rental property for a new condo in Wyoming with an FMV of $68,000. Irene's Montana property isn't as valuable as the condo in Wyoming, so as part of the exchange, Irene pays $20,000 in cash to the owner of the Wyoming property. This is a qualified section 1031 exchange. After the exchange is complete, what is Irene's basis in her new rental property?

A. $17,000
B. $37,000
C. $60,000
D. $68,000

66. Which of the following taxpayers would not be eligible for the Premium Tax Credit?

A. A married individual who is a victim of domestic abuse and files a separate tax return.
B. A taxpayer who was enrolled in a qualified health plan for six months during the taxable year.
C. An individual who received 16 weeks of unemployment compensation during the year.
D. An individual who is not lawfully present in the United States.

67. Dominic is a self-employed professional athlete with several employees. In 2023, his personal assistant sued Dominic for sexual harassment. Rather than risk a public court battle, Dominic paid a confidential settlement to his former employee. The settlement was $20,000 and subject to a nondisclosure agreement. The legal fees Dominic incurred to negotiate the settlement totaled $9,000. How much of the settlement is deductible, and how should Dominic's legal expenses be reported?

A. $0 (none of the amounts are deductible).
B. $20,000 is deductible as a business expense on Schedule C.
C. $29,000 is deductible as a business expense on Schedule C.
D. $20,000 is deductible as a business expense on Schedule C. $9,000 is deductible as an adjustment to income on his Form 1040.

68. Hamilton is 26, unmarried, and still living with his parents. Hamilton worked a regular job and was not a student. He earned $14,950 in wages and provided more than half of his own support. Hamilton does not have any children or other dependents. Based on this information, which credit would Hamilton likely qualify for?

A. Earned Income Tax Credit.
B. Child Tax Credit.
C. American Opportunity Credit.
D. Foreign Tax Credit.

69. Stefan and Delilah are divorced. They have one child together, named Kaylee. Kaylee is 9 years old and lives with Delilah most of the year. Kaylee only visits her father on weekends. Stefan provides over half of his child's overall support and also obtains a signed Form 8332 from Delilah. Stefan will claim his daughter on his tax return this year. Which of the following credits is Stefan eligible for as a *noncustodial* parent?

A. Earned Income Tax Credit.
B. Child Tax Credit.
C. Child and Dependent Care Credit.
D. Other Dependent Credit.

70. Danny incurred the following losses during the year. Which of the following would be a deductible loss on his tax return in 2023?

A. A $2,000 property loss due to progressive deterioration on a shed behind his home.
B. A $3,000 theft loss of personal jewelry from a burglary.
C. A $10,000 loss on stock from a recognized Ponzi scheme.
D. A $5,000 gambling loss from purchasing lottery tickets. Danny did not have any gambling winnings.

71. Ivan and Irina are married and file jointly. They live together in Arkansas. They run a small car wash together, with each working 2,000 hours in the business during the year. The business is not incorporated, not an LLC, and there are no other owners. What are their options for reporting their income and loss from the business?

A. Either as a qualified joint venture or partnership.
B. Sole proprietorship.
C. Corporation.
D. A joint real estate activity.

72. Paulo is age 65 and widowed. He has a 17-year-old son named Kayden. Paulo's wife died two years ago, and he has not remarried. Kayden is a full-time high school student and has lived with his father all year. Paulo will file as a Qualifying Surviving Spouse (QSS) in 2023, claiming his son as a dependent. Paulo does not plan to itemize. What is his standard deduction amount?

A. $12,950
B. $19,400
C. $27,700
D. $29,200

73. Christopher and Patty are married and file jointly. They live and work in Vermont, but they own some foreign investments. Their Form 1099-DIV shows foreign tax paid of $590. They want to claim the Foreign Tax Credit for the foreign income tax that they paid. Are they required to file Form 1116?

A. No, they are not required to file Form 1116.
B. Yes, they are required to complete Form 1116 because foreign taxes must always be reported.
C. Yes, they are required because their foreign taxes have a special reporting requirement.
D. No, they are not required to complete Form 1116 because their foreign taxes are not deductible on their U.S. tax return.

74. Which of the following tests is *not* applicable when determining whether a child is a qualifying child for the purposes of the Earned Income Tax Credit?

A. Age test.
B. Relationship test.
C. Joint return test.
D. Disability test.

75. Which individuals qualify for an automatic 2-month extension to June 15, to file their U.S. income tax return?

A. U.S. citizens residing in Puerto Rico.
B. U.S. residents legally present in the United States.
C. U.S. citizens who work and live abroad.
D. U.S. citizens serving in the military within the United States.

76. Allie converted her home to a residential rental five years ago. On the date she converted the property, her cost basis was $375,000, and the fair market value of the house was $230,000. She had claimed $18,000 of depreciation when she sold the property for $205,000 on February 2, 2023. What is the amount of Allie's deductible loss?

A. $0
B. $7,000
C. $25,000
D. $43,000

77. Which of the following types of income would be "qualifying income" for the purposes of the Earned Income Tax Credit?

A. Taxable alimony.
B. Worker's Compensation.
C. Nontaxable combat pay.
D. Unemployment compensation.

78. Orlando is a self-employed architect. During the tax year, he pays the following fines and penalties. Which of these are deductible as a business expense?

A. Penalties paid to a client for the late performance on a construction contract when the project was not completed by the agreed-upon due date.
B. Parking ticket incurred while he was visiting a client's work location.
C. Penalties for paying his federal income tax late.
D. Penalties for filing his state tax return late.

79. What is the maximum amount that can be claimed for the "Credit for Other Dependents"?

A. $500 per tax return.
B. $500 per qualifying dependent.
C. $500 per taxpayer.
D. $2,500 per tax return.

80. Nicole's AGI is $50,000. All her income is from wages. She donated $2,000 cash to her local church as well as appreciated stock with a current fair market value of $28,000. Her cost basis in the stock was $22,000 (this is what she paid for the stock three years ago). Nicole plans to itemize this year. What is her allowable deduction for charitable gifts on Schedule A?

A. $17,000
B. $24,000
C. $25,000
D. $30,000

81. Which of the following will *not* disqualify a taxpayer from claiming the Lifetime Learning Credit?

A. The taxpayer is claimed as a dependent on someone else's tax return.
B. The taxpayer files as married filing separately.
C. The taxpayer's adjusted gross income (AGI) is above the limit for the taxpayer's filing status.
D. The taxpayer's spouse is a nonresident alien who elects to be treated as a resident alien for tax purposes.

82. Carter is married but files separately from his wife. In 2023, Carter has the following income and losses:

| Income type | Amount |
|---|---|
| Wages from employment | $79,000 |
| Long-term capital LOSS from the sale of stock | ($14,000) |
| Long-term capital GAIN from the sale of land | $7,400 |

Based on the information above, what is his AGI and capital loss carryover for the year?

A. AGI: $72,400, capital loss carryover, $0.
B. AGI: $75,400, capital loss carryover $3,100.
C. AGI: $75,400, capital loss carryover $3,600.
D. AGI: $77,500, capital loss carryover $5,100.

83. Tarah is a full-time college student in her second year of school. She incurs various educational expenses during the year. Which of the following is NOT a qualifying educational expense for the American Opportunity Tax Credit?

A. $200 for a required textbook she bought online.
B. $300 in required supplies for a medical course.
C. $125 in required student health fees.
D. $120 in sports equipment for a physical education course required for her degree.

84. Ana likes to collect antique figurines. She purchased an old figurine at a garage sale two years ago. The figurine cost $25. Later, Ana discovers the figurine is a valuable collectible and lists the toy on U-Bid, an online auction website. Buyers immediately start bidding on the figurine, and it eventually sells for $9,700. U-Bid kept a 10% auction commission on the sale ($970). Ana is not a professional toy dealer and has never sold a toy online before. How should Ana report this sale on her tax return?

A. Ana should report the $9,700 on Schedule C and deduct $970 as a business expense.
B. Ana should report $8,705 as a long-term capital gain on Schedule D (Form 1040).
C. Ana should report $9,700 as a portfolio income on Schedule E (Form 1040).
D. Ana should report $9,675 as a short-term capital gain on Schedule D (Form 1040).

85. Judd is 52 and owns several investments that generate interest income throughout the year. He also has a traditional IRA, to which he makes contributions each year. At the end of the year, he gets statements listing the income earned on each investment. Which of the following types of interest income will have to be reported on his 2023 tax return?

A. Interest earned inside his traditional IRA.
B. Interest received on tax-exempt municipal bonds.
C. Interest on insurance dividends left on deposit with the U.S. Department of Veterans Affairs.
D. Interest on HSA funds (none of the funds in his HSA were withdrawn).

86. Monica, age 32, is single. Her AGI in 2023 is $93,600. Monica incurs $6,200 of qualified out-of-pocket medical expenses during the year. What amount can she deduct as a medical expense on Schedule A (after applying the 7.5% AGI limit)?

A. $0
B. $410
C. $620
D. $6,200

87. Which of the following types of income are *not* subject to the Additional Medicare Tax?

A. Distributions from qualified retirement plans.
B. Tips.
C. Self-employment income.
D. Wages.

88. Shannon claimed the Earned Income Tax Credit in a prior year. The IRS audited her return and determined that she was not eligible to claim the credit and that her EITC claim was fraudulent because she claimed dependents that were unrelated to her. How many years must she wait before claiming the credit again?

A. One year.
B. Two years.
C. Ten years.
D. A taxpayer who is found guilty of fraud related to the EITC can never claim the credit again.

89. Rodney and Crystal are married and have always filed jointly. They do not live in a community property state. Crystal dies on February 27, 2023. Before her death, Crystal had earned $17,500 in wages. Crystal also leaves her husband a $125,000 life insurance policy. Rodney chooses to receive the life insurance proceeds as an annuity. In 2023, he receives $11,100 associated with the life insurance policy ($11,000 policy payout plus $100 in interest). He also earned $32,000 in wages during the year. On December 29, 2023, Rodney remarries. Rodney will file his 2023 return with his new wife, Laura. Laura does not work and does not receive any income during the year. Based on these facts, how much gross income must Rodney include on his 2023 tax return?

A. $32,000
B. $32,100
C. $43,500
D. $58,000

90. Rodolfo is an alcoholic. He enters a treatment facility for alcohol abuse. The treatment costs $24,000. Which of the following statements is true?

A. Rodolfo cannot deduct any of the alcohol treatment costs as a medical expense.
B. Rodolfo can deduct the cost of the alcohol treatment center, including meals and lodging, as a qualified medical expense.
C. Rodolfo can only deduct the cost of alcohol treatment if it is done in a hospital setting.
D. Alcoholism is not recognized by the IRS as a medical condition, and therefore related expenses are not deductible.

91. Angelica is a wealthy investor. She gives a $60,000 cash gift to her favorite nephew at the beginning of the year. On December 1, 2023, Angelica dies. In this scenario, who is responsible for filing the gift tax return and paying the gift tax (if any is due)?

A. No one, because Angelica died.
B. Her nephew, the gift recipient.
C. The executor of Angelica's estate.
D. Whoever is named in Angelica's will as her primary beneficiary.

92. Gerry changed employers on January 3, 2023, and his new employer does not offer health insurance. Gerry plans to apply for insurance through the Healthcare Marketplace, and he wants to know if he qualifies for a subsidy. For the purposes of the Premium Tax Credit, the calculation of Gerry's household income would include which of the following?

A. Supplemental Security Income (SSI).
B. Child support payments.
C. Federal disaster relief assistance payments.
D. Tax-exempt interest.

93. Janessa is single. She is a self-employed jazz musician who operates her business as a sole proprietorship. After applying applicable deductions, she has $80,000 in qualified business income during the year. She also has $40,000 in interest income from various investments. Her total taxable income for the year (before the QBI deduction) is $107,000. What is her maximum qualified business income deduction?

A. $8,000
B. $16,000
C. $18,000
D. $20,000

94. Stacey earns $79,000 in wages in 2023. She is single and has no other taxable income for the year. She pays $14,500 in mortgage interest on her primary residence. She also pays an additional $3,000 in mortgage interest on her second home, a vacation cottage in Utah. She also incurs $12,000 in loan interest on a plot of land that she purchased during the year and intends to build another vacation home on. How much interest can she potentially deduct as an itemized deduction on her Schedule A?

A. $14,500
B. $15,800
C. $17,500
D. $29,500

95. Rupert is a full-time college student. He is in his second year of college in an undergraduate degree program. He had the following expenses in 2023. What are his total qualifying education expenses for the purposes of the American Opportunity Tax Credit?

| College tuition | $4,000 |
| Required textbooks purchased from a friend | $400 |
| Student health fees paid to the college | $125 |
| Room and board | $4,500 |

A. $4,000
B. $4,400
C. $4,525
D. $9,025

96. Henrietta adopted a child this year through a private adoption agency. The child was born in the U.S. and is a U.S. citizen. The child is determined by the state to have special needs. Once the adoption is complete, she determines that she has $4,000 in qualifying adoption expenses. Her income tax liability is $5,000 for the year *before* the application of the adoption credit. How should she apply for the adoption credit?

A. Henrietta is allowed to deduct $4,000 in adoption expenses on her tax return.
B. Henrietta is allowed to take the full adoption credit of $15,950 in 2023; the remaining credit is refundable.
C. Henrietta is not allowed to take the adoption credit because children adopted from private adoption agencies are not eligible for the credit.
D. Henrietta is allowed to take an adoption credit of $5,000 in 2023, and she may carryover her unused adoption credit to future tax years.

97. Kathleen is 80 years old. She is a wealthy widow who likes to donate to several of her favorite charities throughout the year. She has a traditional IRA and is required to take an RMD (required minimum distribution) during the year. She decides to make a tax-free gift directly from her IRA to her church. Her AGI in 2023 is $80,000, and all her income is from passive investments. What is the maximum amount that Kathleen can withdraw from her traditional IRA tax-free as a qualified charitable contribution (QCD)?

A. $0
B. $40,000
C. $80,000
D. $100,000

98. Kiyoshi is single and works as a self-employed web designer. He files a Schedule C. In 2023, he expects to earn approximately $250,000. In 2022 (the prior year), his AGI was $175,000. In order to avoid paying an estimated tax penalty, Kiyoshi can rely on the safe harbor rule for higher-income taxpayers by paying:

A. 90% of the tax liability on his prior-year tax return.
B. 100% of the tax liability on his prior-year tax return.
C. 110% of the tax liability on his prior-year tax return.
D. 150% of the tax liability on his prior-year tax return.

99. Which of the following expenses is NOT allowable as an itemized deduction on Schedule A?

A. Motor vehicle registration fees based on the vehicle's value
B. Mortgage interest on a primary residence.
C. Investment interest expense.
D. Funeral expenses.

100. A *noncustodial* parent may claim a child as a dependent only if the custodial parent releases a claim to exemption using which form?

A. Form 8332.
B. Form 2848.
C. Schedule EIC.
D. Form 1065.

**Please review your answer choices with the correct answers in the next section.**

# Answers to Exam #3: Individuals

**1. The answer is B.** The $20,000 in canceled debt is not taxable to Harold under the qualified principal residence indebtedness exclusion (QPRI exclusion), but it must be reported on Form 982. Since Harold was able to negotiate a workout with his mortgage lender (reducing the amount he owed on the mortgage and staying in the home), he does not have to complete either Form 8949 or Schedule D because he did not dispose of the home. His basis in the home would be decreased by $20,000, as illustrated in the sample form below (this question is based on an example in Publication 4491).

**2. The answer is B.** The rental income received after Jiro's death should be reported on Form 1041. On the date after a taxpayer's death, an estate begins its existence as a separate entity. The rental income received *after* Jiro's death should be reported on Form 1041, not his individual Form 1040. The estate's executor is responsible for filing Jiro's final tax return as well as Form 1041 for his estate.

**3. The answer is A.** Home mortgage interest is only deductible if the mortgage is a <u>secured</u> debt. The loan *must* be secured by the property for the interest to be deductible. Interest paid on unsecured loans (such as credit card debt) is not deductible as mortgage interest. Further, the taxpayer must be legally liable for the debt in order to deduct the mortgage interest. The home does not have to be the taxpayer's main home in order for the mortgage interest to be deductible. A taxpayer may deduct the mortgage interest on a first home and a second home, up to the mortgage loan acquisition limit.

> **Note:** The $750,000 figure relates to the maximum amount of qualified acquisition *debt*, not the amount of interest paid. Also, if the home was purchased on or before December 15, 2017, the qualified acquisition indebtedness limit is "grandfathered" at a higher limit of $1 million ($500,000 MFS).

**4. The answer is C.** Roland must report the full amount of punitive damages as ordinary income. Punitive damages are always taxable. The $625,000 would be reported as ordinary income in the year it is received. The lawyer's fees are not deductible because miscellaneous itemized deductions that were limited by the 2%-of-AGI rule prior to the TCJA are no longer deductible. The $159,000 in compensatory damages for physical injury are not taxable and do not need to be reported on Roland's tax return.[29]

**5. The answer is B.** Aurora and Crispin's *Additional Medicare Tax* is **$720**. Because their *combined* wages exceed $250,000, they owe an additional 0.9% Medicare tax on $80,000 ($330,000 - $250,000). The additional tax due is $720 ($80,000 × .9%). This would have to be paid on their joint tax return because neither Aurora nor Crispin's employer would be responsible for withholding the additional tax on their wages because neither met the $200,000 withholding threshold. A taxpayer is liable for Additional Medicare Tax if the taxpayer's wages or self-employment income (together with that of his or her spouse if filing a joint return) exceed the threshold amount for the individual's filing status:

| Filing Status | Threshold Amount |
|---|---|
| Married filing jointly | $250,000 |
| Married filing separate | $125,000 |
| Single, HOH, Qualifying Surviving Spouse (QSS) | $200,000 |

The *Additional Medicare Tax* was legislated as part of the Affordable Care Act. Under this mandate, in addition to withholding Medicare tax at 1.45%, employers must withhold a 0.9% Additional Medicare Tax from an employee's wages once their earnings reach $200,000 in a calendar year.

---

[29] As a result of the Tax Cuts and Jobs Act, nonbusiness legal fees are generally not deductible through 2025, subject to a few exceptions. Attorney fees incurred in connection with legal claims of unlawful discrimination and certain claims against the federal government are still eligible for a deduction.

**6. The answer is D.** Tax preparation fees are no longer deductible due to the Tax Cuts and Jobs Act. However, a business may deduct accounting and tax expenses (this question is based on an EA exam question released by the IRS).

**7. The answer is C.** Due to changes in the Tax Cuts and Jobs Act, the deduction for personal casualty and theft losses as an itemized deduction has generally been eliminated for personal-use property, with the exception of casualty losses suffered in a federal disaster area. However, casualty losses on business/rental property are still fully deductible, regardless of whether or not it is in a federal disaster area.

**8. The answer is D.** Tammy's filing status is single, so her 2023 standard deduction amount is $13,850 based on her filing status. She is also allowed an "additional" standard deduction for blindness in the amount of $1,850; therefore, her standard deduction in 2023 would be **$15,700** ($13,850 + $1,850). The 2023 standard deduction amounts are as follows:

- Single/MFS: $13,850
- MFJ or Qualifying Surviving Spouse (QSS): $27,700
- Head of Household: $20,800
- If the taxpayer is legally blind and/or 65 or older, the additional standard deduction is:
    - $1,500 for MFS, MFJ or QSS
    - $1,850 for Single and HOH

**9. The answer is C.** In 2023, Taylor qualifies for the Child Tax Credit, and Ginger qualifies for the Credit for Other Dependents. In 2023, in order to qualify for the Child Tax Credit, a child must have been *under* the age of 17. Ginger is a qualifying dependent for the ODC. Qualifying persons for the ODC include qualifying children who are older than the threshold for the Child Tax Credit or qualifying relatives, such as dependent parents.

**10. The answer is B.** Since Anita signed Form 8332, the dependency exemption and the Child Tax Credit are given to Enrique, the *noncustodial* parent. However, Anita can still file as Head of Household and claim the Earned Income Credit based on Juana, as long as she otherwise qualifies for those credits.

**11. The answer is C.** A taxpayer does not need to be living overseas or have a foreign tax home in order to take the Foreign Tax Credit. Generally, the following four tests must be met for any foreign tax to qualify for the Foreign Tax Credit:

- It must be a tax imposed on the taxpayer.
- The taxpayer must have paid or accrued the tax.
- The tax must be the legal and actual foreign tax liability.
- The tax must be an income tax or a tax imposed in lieu of an income tax.

**12. The answer is D.** Penelope must include $19,000 in her income [100 shares × ($200 fair market value – $10 discounted price that she paid)]. Penelope's stock was not substantially vested when it was transferred, so she doesn't have to include any amounts in her income until 2023, because before that date, it was subject to substantial restrictions. For more details on restricted stock, see IRS Publication 525, *Taxable and Nontaxable Income.*

**13. The answer is B.** Thor can make a *non*-deductible contribution to his traditional IRA of $6,500 in 2023. Even if a taxpayer isn't eligible to deduct their traditional IRA contribution on their taxes, as is the case for Thor, as his AGI is too high, many taxpayers still choose to make a non-deductible IRA contribution. Thor's contribution will grow on a tax-deferred basis, despite the fact that it is nondeductible. Form 8606 is used by taxpayers to report nondeductible contributions to their traditional IRAs. He earns too much to make a direct contribution to a Roth IRA. He cannot make a *deductible* contribution to a traditional IRA, but he is allowed to make a nondeductible contribution to a traditional IRA.

**14. The answer is A.** Kirby has qualified principal residence indebtedness (QPRI). The cancellation of debt is not taxable as the $10,000 of forgiven debt (the difference between the amount of the recourse loan at the time of the foreclosure and the home's FMV) was less than the maximum exclusion amount of $750,000 ($375,000 for MFS filers). The debt cancellation must be reported on his individual return. His tax return should include Form 8949 and Schedule D to show both the deemed sales price and the basis of the home disposed of through foreclosure of $185,000 (the FMV at the time of foreclosure) and Form 982 to exclude the $10,000 debt cancellation from income (this question was modified from an example in Publication 4491).

**15. The answer is D.** The exclusion can be claimed by U.S. citizens *and* legal U.S. residents (i.e., green card holders). In order to claim the foreign earned income exclusion, the foreign housing exclusion, or the foreign housing deduction, the taxpayer must:

- Have foreign earned income
- Have a tax home in a foreign country
- Be a bona fide resident of a foreign country or meet the physical presence test in a foreign country or countries
- Make a valid election

**16. The answer is B.** Deductions for *most* entertainment expenses[30] were disallowed by the TCJA, so the tickets to the hockey game would not be deductible. Camilla's only deductible expense was the meal and the transportation to the restaurant. In 2023, businesses can claim 50% of their meal expenses, as long as the expense is not lavish or extravagant. Therefore, **Camilla's deductible expense is $60** [$80 meal × 50% (+ $20 taxi fare)].

---

[30] In general, entertainment expenses are no longer deductible under the Tax Cuts and Jobs Act. However, there are some narrow exceptions for employee events, such as company holiday parties. In addition, any entertainment that is sold to customers, such as a musical performer in a nightclub, would still be fully deductible as a business expense.

**17. The answer is C.** Gambling winnings are reported on Form W-2G. Gambling income includes winnings from lotteries, raffles, horse races, and casinos. It also includes cash winnings and the fair market value of prizes, such as cars, or trips.

**18. The answer is C.** Jennifer and Colton can claim an adoption credit of $31,900 in 2023 ($15,950 per child). The maximum adoption tax credit is $15,950 per child in 2023. In 2023, taxpayers with a modified adjusted gross income below $239,230 can claim the full credit. The adoption credit phases out completely once the taxpayer's income exceeds $279,230. The phaseout limits are the same for every filing status. The adoption credit is claimed on Form 8839, Qualified Adoption Expenses.

**19. The answer is A.** Murray can claim the Educator Expense Deduction, but only for $220 of his expenses. Expenses that qualify for the Educator Expense Deduction (previously, this was called the "Teacher Credit") include books, supplies (including personal protective equipment and other items used to help prevent the spread of COVID-19), equipment (including educational software), and other materials used in the classroom. Expenses for homeschooling, nonathletic supplies for physical education, or health courses do not qualify. In 2023, an eligible educator can deduct up to $300 of qualifying expenses. If the taxpayer and spouse are both educators, they can deduct up to $600. Teachers can deduct these expenses even if they do not itemize deductions. Only certain teachers qualify. An eligible educator must work at least 900 hours a year in a school that provides elementary or secondary education (K-12). The term "educator" includes:

- Teacher
- Instructor or coach
- Counselor
- Principal
- Teacher's aide

The school can be a private school or a public school, but homeschooling expenses do not qualify. College instructors also do not qualify.

**20. The answer is A.** Abel, Imelda, and Martina all qualify for the $500 ODC. The *Credit for Other Dependents* is a non-refundable tax credit of up to $500 per qualifying person. Each dependent must be a U.S citizen, U.S. national, or resident of the U.S. The dependent must have a valid tax identification number (ATIN, ITIN, or SSN). Unlike the Child Tax Credit, the dependent is not required to have a valid SSN (an ITIN or ATIN is allowable) for the taxpayer to claim the credit. The $500 non-refundable credit covers dependents who wouldn't qualify for the Child Tax Credit (such as elderly parents or grandparents).

> **Note:** None of the dependents would qualify for the Child Tax Credit. Abel would not because he is over the age limit for the Child Tax Credit. Imelda would not, because she does not have a valid SSN, and Martina would not, because she is a dependent parent, not a dependent child.

**21. The answer is B.** Beckett's deductible business expense would be calculated as follows: $300 + $245 + $450 + $20 meals (there is a 50% business meal deduction in 2023) = **$1,015**. The golf outing would be classified as "entertainment," so it would not be deductible at all.

**22. The answer is C.** Arlene must report the sale of digital assets on Schedule D and Form 8949. In 2023, a box must be checked on page 1 of her Form 1040 to note that she had a digital asset transaction during the year. Digital assets, such as cryptocurrency, are treated as "property" for U.S. federal tax purposes. Gain on the sale of a digital asset is treated as a capital gain and is netted with other capital gains and losses. Capital gains and losses for individual taxpayers are reported by using Schedule D and Form 8949.

**23. The answer is D.** Holton will not have to pay a penalty because he returned all the money to the IRA within 60 days. The withdrawal and redeposit occurred within the 60-day rollover period. Although "loans" are not allowable from a traditional IRA, essentially, once a taxpayer takes a distribution from their account, the taxpayer will not owe penalties if the full amount is redeposited into a qualified retirement account within 60 days. This would be classified as an "indirect" rollover. Taxpayers are limited to one indirect rollover per year.

**24. The answer is A.** Benito has made an excess contribution of $6,500. He must withdraw the excess contribution (as well as any earnings on the contribution) from his IRA accounts by the filing deadline, or he will be subject to a penalty. Taxpayers are permitted to contribute to both traditional and Roth IRAs in the same year; however, the annual contribution limit applies to both types of IRAs. For 2023, the IRA contribution limit is $6,500 ($7,500 for those taxpayers who are age 50 and older), and it applies to all of a taxpayer's IRA accounts.

**25. The answer is D.** The Premium Tax Credit is designed to make health insurance premiums more affordable. The Premium Tax Credit is based on a taxpayer's estimated household income. The credit amounts are paid directly to the taxpayer's health insurance provider every month.

**26. The answer is B.** Samuel must report and pay tax on all his income, regardless of whether or not he received a 1099-NEC for the income. All of his income should be reported on his Schedule C.

**27. The answer is A.** Waverly is not entitled to the qualified business income deduction, because her business is an SSTB, and her modified taxable income is above the threshold for her filing status. The 199A deduction is subject to certain income limitations. The 199A SSTB phaseouts (based on modified taxable income) for 2023 are as follows:

- Married Filing Joint: $364,200-$464,200
- All other filing statuses: $182,100-$232,100

Her business is a Specified Service Trade or Business[31] and she is single. Her pre-QBI deduction modified taxable income is above the full phaseout of the QBI deduction threshold. Therefore, she is not allowed to take the QBI deduction.

**28. The answer is D.** Sampson can contribute a maximum of $7,500 to a traditional IRA in 2023. The annual IRA contribution limit in 2023 is $6,500 for adults under 50 and $7,500 for adults 50 and older. Since Sampson is over the age of 50, he can contribute $7,500. There is no longer an age limit on making regular contributions to traditional or Roth IRAs. However, Roth IRAs do have an income limitation. The 2023 Roth IRA contribution limit phaseout (MAGI) are as follows:

- $218,000–$228,000: MFJ/QSS
- $138,000–$153,000: Single, HOH, MFS (if did not live with spouse)
- $0 to $10,000: MFS (if lived with a spouse)

Since Sampson earned more than the Roth phaseout limit for his filing status, he cannot make a direct contribution to a Roth IRA.[32]

**29. The answer is B.** A child <u>under the age of 17</u> and claimed as a dependent would be a qualifying child. In order to qualify for the Child Tax Credit, the dependent must be *under* the age of 17 at the end of the year and claimed on the taxpayer's return.[33]

---

[31] A Specified service trade or business (SSTB), includes a trade or business involving the performance of services in the fields of health, law, accounting, actuarial science, performing arts, consulting, athletics, financial services, investing and investment management, securities trading (stockbrokers and dealers), dealing in certain assets, or endorsements.

[32] As part of the SECURE Act, which was enacted in 2019, there is no longer a maximum age at which taxpayers can make a contribution to a traditional or Roth IRA. However, income limits continue to apply to Roth IRAs.

[33] The American Rescue Plan Act (ARPA) had expanded the credit to include a qualifying child that was under 18 years old at the end of the year for the 2021 tax year, but this provision expired in 2022 and was not extended.

**30. The answer is A.** The canceled debt is not taxable to Carly (or her estate or her heirs). While the Tax Cuts and Jobs Act modified the exclusion of student loan discharges on account of death or disability starting back in 2018, under the *American Rescue Plan Act,* most student loan forgiveness is now nontaxable through 2025. [34]

**31. The answer is C.** The interest received on a municipal bond issued by a state or local agency or organization is tax-exempt. These are usually called "muni bonds." Municipal bond funds are one of a few investments on the market that offer exemption from federal tax.

**32. The answer is B.** Heidi has a long-term capital gain of $31,000 on the sale ($91,000 sale price - $60,000 transferred basis). In the case of a gift where the donor's basis is used, the holding period "tacks on" to produce, in this case, a long-term capital gain.

**33. The answer is C.** Vienna's MAGI is below the threshold where the student loan interest deduction is limited below the maximum deduction of $2,500. Therefore, Vienna can deduct $2,500 of her student loan interest as an adjustment to income on her individual return. The maximum amount per return is $2,500, regardless of filing status, so the amount she paid over $2,500 is lost. The 2023 phaseout limits are as follows:

- MFJ: $155,000-$185,000
- Single, HOH, QSS: $75,000-$90,000

Taxpayers with modified adjusted gross income above the thresholds listed above will be phased out from taking the student loan interest deduction. MFS filers cannot take the student loan interest deduction.

**34. The answer is A.** Broderick's qualified hazardous duty pay is not taxable. For U.S. armed forces personnel, taxable income does not include qualified hazardous duty pay. The compensation received for active service in a combat zone (combat pay), or qualified hazardous duty area (hazardous duty pay) is not taxable. All the other payments would be taxable, even if the individual was in a combat zone when he received them. (See Publication 3, *Armed Forces' Tax Guide,* for more information on this topic).

**35. The answer is A.** All of the gain from the sale of Kenny and Glynda's home is excludable. IRC Section 121 allows the exclusion of a capital gain of up to $250,000 ($500,000, if married filing jointly) from the sale of the taxpayer's main home. Although there are some exceptions, in general, the taxpayer must have lived and owned the house for at least two years out of the previous five years before the sale. Since Kenny and Glynda owned and lived in the home for at least two years, all of their gain is excludable from income.

---

[34] Almost all student loans will qualify for forgiveness; one of the following must be applicable to the loan: 1) A loan for postsecondary educational expenses, 2) A private education loan. 3) A loan from an educational organization described in section 170(b)(1)(A)(ii), or 4) A loan from an organization exempt from tax under section 501(a) to refinance a student loan.

**36. The answer is D.** Rebecca is a statutory *non*-employee. Beemer Realty would issue Rebecca a Form 1099-NEC for commissions, and Rebecca would file Schedule C to report her income and expenses. There are generally two categories of statutory nonemployees: direct sellers and licensed real estate agents. They are treated as self-employed for all federal tax purposes, including income and employment taxes, if:

- Substantially all payments for their services as direct sellers or real estate agents are directly related to sales or other output, rather than to the number of hours worked.
- Their services are performed under a written contract providing that they will not be treated as employees for federal tax purposes.

**37. The answer is C.** Taxpayers must use Form 1095-A to complete Form 8962, *Premium Tax Credit*, to reconcile advance payments of the premium tax credit or claim the premium tax credit on their tax return.

**38. The answer is D.** The *first* thing that Debbie should do is contact her employer. If she does not receive her Form W-2 after a reasonable amount of time, she should contact the IRS for assistance, but not before February 15. If she does not receive her Form W-2 by the due date of her return (April 15 for the 2023 tax year), she may file using Form 4852, Substitute for Form W-2, *Wage and Tax Statement*. However, Form 4852 should only be used as a last resort.

**39. The answer is D.** The wages and the scholarship are both taxable to Ximena. She should report the taxable scholarship as "other income" on line 8r of Schedule 1 (Form 1040). A scholarship is generally tax-free if the student is a degree candidate, and the scholarship is used to pay for tuition and required fees. However, Ximena did not attend college, and she used the scholarship to purchase a personal vehicle. Therefore, the entire scholarship is taxable.

**40. The answer is B.** The $50,000 of canceled mortgage debt on a vacation home would be taxable and reportable as canceled debt income. A taxpayer whose debt is canceled, forgiven, or discharged will generally receive a Form 1099-C, Cancellation of Debt, from the creditor. The canceled amount must be included in gross income unless it qualifies for an exception to inclusion (such as cancellation of qualified principal residence indebtedness). The following types of canceled debt would be excluded from gross income:

- Debt canceled in a Title 11 bankruptcy case.
- Debt canceled during insolvency (but only to the extent of the insolvency).
- Cancellation of qualified farm indebtedness.
- Cancellation of qualified real property business indebtedness.
- Cancellation of debt on a primary residence up to $750,000 ($375,000 if MFS).
- Cancellation of student loan debt (under the American Recovery Plan Act, most student loan forgiveness is now nontaxable through 2025).

**41. The answer is D.** The impairment-related work expenses of a disabled employee are still deductible on Schedule A as a miscellaneous itemized deduction. The Tax Cuts and Jobs Act suspended the deduction for miscellaneous itemized deductions that previously were subject to the 2% of AGI limitation. However, there are still some miscellaneous itemized deductions that are allowable. The following deductions are still permitted (and not subject to an AGI limitation):

- Gambling losses (but only to the extent of gambling winnings)
- Casualty and theft losses of income-producing property
- Amortizable premium on taxable bonds
- Federal estate tax on income in respect of a decedent
- Deductions for amortizable bond premium.
- An ordinary loss attributable to a contingent payment debt instrument or an inflation-indexed debt instrument
- Deduction for repayment of amounts under a claim of right if over $3,000
- Certain unrecovered investment in a pension
- Impairment-related work expenses of a disabled person
- Theft losses from Ponzi investment schemes (Form 4684)

**42. The answer is B.** The only income that would be subject to the Net Investment Income tax would be the mutual fund distribution. The NIIT also applies to the following income:

- Interest and dividend
- Capital gains
- Rent and royalty income
- Non-qualified annuities
- Passive income from businesses (such as a limited partnership investment)

The NIIT does not apply to earned income (wages, self-employment income, etc.), taxable alimony, pension income, Social Security, distributions from IRAs, or tax-exempt municipal bond interest.

**43. The answer is B.** Frank's contributions to a Coverdell Education Savings Account (or a similar educational savings plan) are not tax-deductible. A Coverdell ESA is a trust account set up to pay qualified education expenses for a designated beneficiary. The contributions to an educational savings account grow tax-free, but they are not deductible. All of the other contributions listed would be tax-deductible.

**44. The answer is A.** A full-time student for IRS purposes is one "enrolled for some part of five calendar months" at a qualifying school. The five calendar months do not have to be consecutive. The definition of "school" includes a college, technical school, or mechanical school. This information is found in *Publication 17, Your Federal Income Tax.*

160

**45. The answer is D.** Sebastian can contribute $7,500 to his retirement account (because he is over 50). Ruby can contribute $6,500 as long as they file jointly. This is because Sebastian can make a spousal IRA contribution because he has enough qualifying compensation to cover both contributions. Note that this does not apply if the spouses are filing MFS. If Sebastian and Ruby decided to file separate returns, they could both still make a contribution, but Ruby's contribution would be limited by her qualifying compensation ($2,000). In 2023, the IRA contribution limit is $6,500 per person ($7,500 if the taxpayer is 50 or older).

**46. The answer is C.** Kenneth's IRA withdrawal will be subject to income tax but will not be subject to an early withdrawal penalty, because Kenneth has become permanently disabled. The IRA trustee will send Kenneth a 1099-R to report the withdrawal. The distribution code in box 7 of Kenneth's Form 1099-R would be code 3, for "disability."[35]

**47. The answer is B.** Dharma has $9,450 in qualified medical expenses. See the table below. The teeth whitening, prescription medications from other countries, life insurance premiums, and health club dues are not qualifying medical expenses. All of the other expenses listed are specifically permitted. To see a full list of qualifying medical expenses, see *Publication 502, Medical and Dental Expenses.*

| Medical expenses | Amount | Deductible? | Calculation |
|---|---|---|---|
| Teeth Whitening | $500 | No | $0 |
| Prescription medicines from other countries | $1,200 | No | $0 |
| Insulin | $300 | Yes | $300 |
| Health Club Dues | $500 | No | $0 |
| Life insurance premiums | $400 | No | $0 |
| Vision Correction Surgery | $6,700 | Yes | $6,700 |
| Dental insurance premiums | $2,000 | Yes | $2,000 |
| Smoking-cessation program | $450 | Yes | $450 |
| **Total qualified medical expenses** | | | **$9,450** |

---

[35] If the taxpayer is disabled and does not provide proof at the time of the withdrawal, the taxpayer can still file Form 5329 and use the disability "penalty exception" by indicating the penalty exception on their individual Form 1040 at the time of filing.

**48. The answer is C.** Jasper must be physically present in a foreign country (or multiple foreign countries, if he lives in more than one) for at least 330 full days during a period of 12 consecutive months to meet the "physical presence test" for the foreign earned income exclusion. The 330 qualifying days do not have to be consecutive, and they do not have to occur in the same foreign nation. The physical presence test is based only on how long a taxpayer stays in a foreign country. The physical presence test only applies to U.S. citizens and U.S. resident aliens.

**49. The answer is A.** Taxpayers with an interest in (or signature authority over) foreign financial accounts whose aggregate value exceeded $10,000 at any time during the year generally must file an FBAR. This requirement exists whether the taxpayer lives in the U.S. or abroad, and it applies to every U.S. person (U.S. citizens, green card holders, and resident aliens). Foreign accounts include bank accounts, securities accounts, and certain foreign retirement arrangements (such as a foreign pension). The FBAR must be filed electronically through FinCEN's BSA E-Filing System (it is not filed with the IRS or with the taxpayer's individual return). Although the FBAR is not filed with the IRS, the IRS is responsible for FBAR enforcement.

**50. The answer is D.** Crop insurance proceeds of $600 or more would be reported to the taxpayer on Form 1099-MISC. Answer "A" is incorrect because nonemployee compensation is reported on Form 1099-NEC. Answer "B" is incorrect because canceled debt is reported on Form 1099-C. Answer "C" is incorrect because interest income is reported on Form 1099-INT. See the Form 1099-MISC instructions for more information.

**51. The answer is C.** Home equity loan interest that is not used to "buy, build or substantially improve a home" is no longer deductible as mortgage interest on Schedule A. Answer "A" is incorrect because the deduction for investment *interest* expense is still allowable (although the deduction for investment expenses has been repealed by the Tax Cuts and Jobs Act). Answers "B" and "D" are incorrect because the mortgage interest paid on a first and second home is deductible on Schedule A, up to the acquisition debt limit.

**52. The answer is A.** Since Ashton and Moana converted the home to a rental property, and it is no longer their primary residence, they must pay the entire unpaid balance of the credit. The First-Time Homebuyer Credit is repaid as an additional tax on a taxpayer's return if the taxpayer bought their home and took the credit in 2008. It works out to annual repayments of $500 per year on a 15-year repayment period. To repay the credit, the taxpayer must attach a completed Form 5405, *First-Time Homebuyer Credit and Repayment of the Credit*, to their federal tax return.

> **Note:** If a taxpayer dies before the repayment is completed, then the remainder of the credit does not need to be paid back. If a married couple purchases a home together and one spouse subsequently dies before the 15-year repayment period ends, the survivor is responsible for only one-half of the repayment balance. The portion owed by the deceased spouse is effectively forgiven.

**53. The answer is C.** Egbert's base amount for figuring the taxable portion of Social Security is $25,000. In general, taxpayers who file MFS get a base amount of $0, *except* when the taxpayer lives apart from his spouse for the entire tax year. The base amounts are:

- $32,000 for MFJ.
- $25,000 for taxpayers filing as Single, HOH, or Qualifying Surviving Spouse (QSS).
- $0 for MFS (but taxpayers who file MFS and live apart from their spouses for the entire year may use the higher rate of $25,000 for "single" taxpayers).

**54. The answer is B.** Pearl would not include the life insurance proceeds in the calculation because life insurance proceeds are not taxable to the beneficiary and not included in the calculation of taxable Social Security. To calculate whether Social Security benefits may be taxable, the taxpayer must compare the "base amount" for their filing status with the total of:

- One-half of their Social Security benefits; plus
- All other income, *including* tax-exempt interest.

All of the other income listed must be included in the calculation. See IRS Publication 17 for more information (this question was modified from an EA exam question released by Prometric).

**55. The answer is B.** Courtney's total allowable deductions on Schedule A are $17,300. Most employee-related unreimbursed work expenses are no longer deductible.[36] Courtney's gambling losses are only deductible to the extent of the gambling winnings ($3,000). The TCJA established a new limit on the amount of state and local taxes (SALT) that can be deducted on Schedule A. The itemized deduction for state and local taxes paid is capped at $10,000 per return for single filers, HOH filers, and MFJ (the cap is $5,000 for married taxpayers filing separately). Since Courtney is filing MFS, her SALT deduction is capped at $5,000. The answer is calculated as follows:

| Type of Expense | Actual | Reason | Allowable |
|---|---|---|---|
| Mortgage interest on main home | $6,700 | Allowable | $6,700 |
| Property tax on main home | $5,300 | Allowable up to $5,000 | $5,000 |
| Misc. unreimbursed work expenses | $5,200 | Not allowable | $0 |
| Charitable donation to a church | $2,600 | Allowable | $2,600 |
| Gambling losses | $6,600 | Limited gambling winnings | $3,000 |
| **Allowable deductions on Schedule A** | | | **$17,300** |

---

[36] Military reservists, qualified performing artists, and fee-basis state and local government officials can still deduct certain job-related expenses. Certain other miscellaneous itemized expenses that were not subject to the 2%-of-AGI deduction are also still allowable, including impairment-related work expenses (work-related expenses incurred by a disabled individual relating to their disability, such as the purchase of a magnifying screen for a person with low vision).

**56. The answer is A.** Contributions to a Traditional IRA are deductible. Answer "B" and "C" are incorrect, because contributions to a Roth are not deductible, as they are made with pre-tax funds. Answer "D" is incorrect because a Coverdell ESA (also known as an Education IRA) is a type of educational savings account to help families save for college expenses. Contributions to a Coverdell are not deductible.

**57. The answer is A.** Jada's modified adjusted gross income is $195,000 ($45,000 wages + $150,000 in taxable capital gains). Since her modified adjusted gross income is below the threshold amount of $200,000, she does not owe any Net Investment Income Tax.

**58. The answer is B.** The election may be ended if Bertrand dies, because the election may be ended due to: revocation of the choice, death, divorce, legal separation, or inadequate records. The default filing status for a U.S. citizen married to a nonresident alien spouse is Married Filing Separately (MFS). However, the spouses can elect to file jointly by making an election with their joint tax return. The election to treat a nonresident alien spouse as a resident alien applies to all later years unless suspended or ended. The election may be suspended during a later year if neither spouse is a U.S. citizen nor a resident alien during that year.

**59. The answer is D.** Although subject to an AGI limit for regular tax purposes, charitable contributions are not an AMT "preference item," which means that, even if a taxpayer is subject to the AMT, their charitable contributions will continue to reduce their tax liability, up to the AGI limit for charitable contributions. The TCJA substantially changed the AMT for individual taxpayers (the corporate AMT was completely repealed). The TCJA increased the AMT exemption for all filing statuses. The AMT exemption amount in 2023 has increased to $81,300 ($63,250 for MFS and $126,500 for MFJ or QSS). AMT exemptions phase out at 25¢ per dollar earned once a taxpayer's AMTI hits a certain threshold. In 2023, the exemption starts phasing out at $578,150 in AMTI for single filers and $1,156,300 for MFJ. Taxpayers who are subject to the AMT must compute their Alternative Minimum Tax on Form 6251, which is attached to their Form 1040.

**60. The answer is B.** Ursula must report her nonqualified dividends on Schedule B and they will be taxed as ordinary income. Unlike qualified dividends, nonqualified dividends are taxed at higher ordinary income tax rates. Qualified dividends are taxed at long-term capital gains rates (which are lower). Dividends are reported to the taxpayer on Form 1099-DIV, "Dividends and Distributions," from the financial institution. Taxpayers must use Schedule B, *Interest and Ordinary Dividends*, to report their dividend and interest earnings if the combined total exceeds $1,500.

**61. The answer is A.** Form W-4, *Employee's Withholding Allowance Certificate* is used by individual taxpayers to change their withholding with their employers. An employee can submit a new Form W-4 each year if they wish, or whenever their personal or financial situation changes.

**62. The answer is B.** Everly cannot deduct medical expenses that were already paid with a tax-free distribution from her HSA. Answer "A" is incorrect because personal casualty losses are still deductible if the loss occurs in a federally declared disaster area. Answer "C" is incorrect because a charitable gift to a veteran's organization is deductible. Answer "D" is incorrect because sales taxes can be deducted on Schedule A. The taxpayer has the option of claiming *either* state and local income taxes or state and local sales taxes (they can't claim both).

**63. The answer is B.** Only the charitable mileage would be deductible for Lynne in 2023. The allowable rate in 2023 is 14 cents per mile driven in service of a charitable organization. Lynne cannot deduct the commuting miles or the unreimbursed mileage that she incurred running errands for her employer. Moving expenses, including mileage related to moving, are not deductible in 2023 *except* for active-duty military personnel. In 2023, the standard mileage rates are:

- 65.5 cents per mile for business miles[37]
- 22 cents per mile driven for medical or Armed Forces moving purposes
- 14 cents per mile driven in service of charitable organizations

Based on the information given, the calculations for Lynne's deductible miles are as follows:

| Type of Mileage | Miles | Calculation | Deduction |
|---|---|---|---|
| Mileage while volunteering | 700 | 14¢ × 700 | $98 |
| Mileage incurred running errands for her employer | 125 | Disallowed | $0 |
| Commuting mileage from her home to her regular workplace | 2,900 | Disallowed | $0 |
| Mileage incurred while moving due to a job transfer | 1,200 | Disallowed | $0 |
| **Allowable deductions on Schedule A** | | | **$98** |

**64. The answer is C.** Della may file as *single*, claiming her daughter as a dependent, and claim the EITC. Geraldine is a qualifying child of both Della and Layton because Geraldine meets the dependency tests for both of them. However, only one taxpayer can claim the child as a dependent. A custodial parent always has the primary right to claim their own child. However, since Della did not pay the costs of keeping up the home, she does not qualify for head of household filing status.

**65. The answer is B.** The basis of Irene's new (Wyoming) property is **$37,000** (equal to the adjusted basis of the old property, $17,000, *plus* the additional cash she paid, $20,000). If a taxpayer trades property in a like-kind exchange and also pays money (also called "boot"), the basis of the property received is the adjusted basis of the property given up, increased by the money they paid to the other party.

---

[37] The standard mileage rate for business cannot be used to claim an itemized deduction for unreimbursed employee travel expenses during the suspension of miscellaneous itemized deductions that are subject to the 2% of AGI floor under the Tax Cuts and Jobs Act.

**66. The answer is D.** No PTC is allowed for an individual who is not lawfully present in the United States. The other taxpayers listed could qualify for the Premium Tax Credit (PTC). The Premium Tax Credit is a tax credit designed to make insurance premiums more affordable to individuals that enroll in a plan through the Health Insurance Marketplace.

**67. The answer is A.** Dominic cannot deduct his legal fees or the amount of the settlement, either as a business expense or any other type of deduction. A taxpayer cannot deduct any settlement or payment related to sexual harassment or sexual abuse if the settlement is subject to a nondisclosure agreement. A business also cannot deduct attorney fees related to such a settlement or payment. See Publication 334, *Tax Guide for Small Business,* for more information.

**68. The answer is A.** Hamilton would likely qualify for the Earned Income Tax Credit. His parents can't claim him because he provides more than one-half of his own support, and he does not meet the age test for a qualifying child. So, he must file as "single." Hamilton can claim the Earned Income Tax Credit (EITC) even if he doesn't have a qualifying child for the EITC, as long as he has earned income and his income is under the threshold amounts.

| Children Claimed | Maximum AGI in 2023 Single, HOH, or QSS | Maximum AGI (MFJ filers) |
|---|---|---|
| Zero ("childless EITC") | $17,640 | $24,210 |
| One | $46,560 | $53,120 |
| Two | $52,918 | $59,478 |
| Three or more | $56,838 | $63,698 |

**69. The answer is B.** Stefan may claim the Child Tax Credit, because the Child Tax Credit can be claimed by a *noncustodial* parent. However, a *noncustodial* parent cannot claim EITC for a child, even if the parent has been given permission to claim a child as a dependent by the custodial parent, because the child must meet the "residency test" for the qualifying child for the purposes of the EITC. Only the custodial parent may claim the Child and Dependent Care Credit. For more information, see Publication 501, *Exemptions, Standard Deduction, and Filing Information.*

**70. The answer is C.** The IRS allows victims of Ponzi schemes to deduct their losses. These losses can be deducted as theft losses (rather than capital losses) using Form 4684. This deduction is not subject to AGI limits.[38] Answer "A" is not correct because losses from progressive deterioration are not deductible. Answer "B" is not correct because personal theft losses are not deductible unless incurred in a federally declared disaster. Answer "D" is incorrect because gambling losses are only deductible up to gambling winnings. Since Danny did not have any gambling winnings, he cannot deduct any of his losses.

---

[38] Revenue Procedure 2009-20 contains a safe harbor that allows taxpayers to deduct up to 95% of a loss when investors have no potential third-party recovery. Ponzi scheme losses are deductible in the year of discovery.

**71. The answer is A.** Ivan and Irina can treat their joint business as either a "qualified joint venture" or as a partnership. If a married couple each materially participates in a jointly-owned and operated business, and the spouses file a joint return for the tax year, they can make a joint election to have the business treated as a "qualified joint venture" instead of a partnership (which is the default tax classification) for the tax year. To make this election, the couple must divide all items of income and loss, and file a separate Schedule C and a separate Schedule SE for each spouse. Making this election allows the taxpayers to avoid the complexity of Form 1065 but still gives each spouse credit for social security earnings on which retirement benefits are based. This election is only available to married taxpayers who file jointly. See Publication 334, *Tax Guide for Small Business,* for more information on qualified joint ventures.

**72. The answer is D.** The correct filing status for Paulo is "Qualifying Surviving Spouse," or "QSS" which has a standard deduction amount of $27,700 (the same as MFJ). He is also allowed an "additional" standard deduction of $1,500 in 2023 for being age 65. Therefore, his standard deduction in 2023 would be **$29,200** ($27,700+ $1,500). The 2023 standard deduction amounts are as follows:

- Single/MFS: $13,850
- MFJ or Qualifying Surviving Spouse (QSS): $27,700
- Head of Household: $20,800
- If the taxpayer is legally blind and/or 65 or older, the additional standard deduction is:
    - $1,500 for MFS, MFJ or QSS
    - $1,850 for Single and HOH

**73. The answer is A.** Christopher and Patty are not required to complete Form 1116 because their foreign taxes are less than $600 in 2023. They may still claim the Foreign Tax Credit. Taxpayers can claim the Foreign Tax Credit directly on Schedule 3 of Form 1040 (without filing any additional forms) if, among other conditions, all foreign income is specified passive category income and total foreign taxes paid do not exceed $300 ($600 MFJ). See Publication 514, *Foreign Tax Credit for Individuals*, for more information about the foreign tax credit.

**74. The answer is D.** There is no such thing as a "disability test" for a qualifying child, although there is a component to the "age test" that allows a taxpayer to claim a child of any age if the child is permanently disabled. The five tests for a qualifying child for the purposes of the Earned Income Tax Credit are:

1. Age test
2. Relationship test
3. Residency test
4. Joint Return test
5. Tie-breaker test

See Publication 596, *Earned Income Credit,* for more information.

**75. The answer is C.** An automatic 2-month extension to June 15 is granted to U.S. citizens and resident aliens that live and work overseas. This extension also applies to military servicemembers on active duty outside the U.S. (but not those stationed within the United States). In cases where the deadline falls on a weekend or holiday, it is pushed back to the next business day.

**76. The answer is B.** Allie has a loss on the sale of the rental property, calculated as follows:

($230,000 FMV on the date of conversion - $18,000 depreciation) = $212,000 tax basis
($212,000 tax basis - $205,000 sale price) = **$7,000 loss**

A loss from the sale of a primary residence is not deductible. However, if a primary residence is later converted to a rental, the loss is generally deductible. The loss is calculated on the adjusted tax basis of the rental property. The basis of the converted property is the *lesser* of the:

- The cost basis when the property is placed in service as a rental, or
- The fair market value when it is placed in service.

The adjusted basis is the basis at the *date of conversion* plus any improvements that were made while the property was a rental, minus any depreciation.

**77. The answer is C.** Nontaxable combat pay is considered "earned income" for the purposes of the Earned Income Credit. For purposes of the EITC, earned income includes:

- Wages, salaries, tips,
- Jury duty pay,
- Union strike benefits,
- Long-term disability benefits received prior to minimum retirement age,
- Net earnings from self-employment,
- Statutory employee pay,
- Nontaxable combat pay,
- Qualified Medicare waiver payments.[39]

> **Note:** Although combat pay and qualified Medicare waiver payments are generally not taxable, the taxpayer can *elect* to have the income included in the calculation of the Earned Income Tax Credit if it gives them a better tax result.

**78. The answer is A.** Orlando can deduct the penalties for late performance (or non-performance) on a business contract. These expenses are deductible. Penalties or fines paid to any government entity because of a violation of laws or regulations are not deductible. Penalties for late federal income tax are never deductible.

---

[39] Medicaid waiver payments, as described in IRS Notice 2014-7, are payments under a Medicaid waiver program to an individual care provider who performs certain services, such as meal preparation, laundry, and personal care services, for an eligible person who has the same home as the provider.

**79. The answer is B.** The Credit for Other Dependents (also called the "Other Dependent Credit") is a non-refundable tax credit of up to $500 per qualifying person. Each dependent must be a U.S. citizen, U.S. national, or resident of the U.S. The dependent must have a valid tax identification number (ATIN, ITIN, or SSN). Unlike the Child Tax Credit, the dependent is not required to have a valid SSN (an ITIN or ATIN is allowable) for the taxpayer to claim the credit. The $500 non-refundable credit covers dependents who wouldn't qualify for the Child Tax Credit, such as children who are age 17 and over or dependents with other relationships (such as elderly parents or grandparents).

**80. The answer is A.** Nicole's deduction is limited to **$17,000** ($2,000 + $15,000). The $2,000 cash donated to the church is fully deductible. However, the contribution of appreciated property (the stock) is subject to a 30%-of-AGI limit. Therefore, her deduction for the appreciated stock is limited to $15,000 (30% limitation × $50,000 AGI). The unused part of the gift ($13,000) can be carried over to future tax years. Nicole may deduct the excess contributions in each of the next 5 years until it is used up, but not beyond that time.

**81. The answer is D.** If a taxpayer (or spouse) *elects* to be treated as a resident alien for tax purposes, he can be eligible for the Lifetime Learning Credit. The following disqualifies a taxpayer from eligibility for education credits:

- The taxpayer is claimed as a dependent on someone else's tax return.
- The taxpayer files as married filing separately.
- The taxpayer's income is above the phaseout limits for the taxpayer's filing status.
- The taxpayer (or spouse) is a nonresident alien for any part of the tax year and *did not elect* to be treated as a resident alien for tax purposes.

**82. The answer is D.** The capital gains and losses are first netted against each other, leaving Carter an overall capital loss for the year of $6,600. Capital losses can be deducted against wages and other income, but only up to a certain limit. Normally, taxpayers can deduct up to $3,000 of capital losses against other kinds of income. However, taxpayers who file MFS are only allowed to deduct one-half of the normal limit ($1,500). Any remaining capital losses can be carried over to subsequent tax years (until the taxpayer's death). The capital loss carryover is calculated as follows:

| | |
|---|---|
| Long-term capital loss from the sale of stock | ($14,000) |
| Long-term capital gain from the sale of land | $7,400 |
| Net capital loss for the year | ($6,600) |
| MFS capital loss limit | $1,500 |
| **Capital loss carryover** | **($5,100)** |

After the capital losses are calculated, $1,500 in capital losses can be deducted from Carter's wages to arrive at AGI ($79,000 - $1,500 = **$77,500**).

**83. The answer is C.** Tarah cannot use the student health fees as an educational expense. The student health fees are not qualifying expenses, even if the cost is required by the educational institution. For the American Opportunity Tax Credit (AOTC), qualified educational expenses include only expenditures for required course materials, as well as tuition and required fees. The cost of a required textbook bought from an off-campus bookstore or online store is a qualified education expense. The following expenses do not qualify for the AOTC:

- Room and board (including the cost of dormitory housing, even if it is required).
- Transportation and insurance.
- Medical expenses (including student health fees).
- Any expenses paid or reimbursed with tax-free educational assistance, such as a scholarship.
- Expenses for sports, games, hobbies or non-credit courses do not qualify for the education credits or tuition and fees deduction, *except* when the course is part of the student's degree program.

**84. The answer is B.** Ana should report **$8,705** as a long-term capital gain on Schedule D (Form 1040). This is the sale of a collectible, which means that the gain will be taxed at her ordinary tax rate (up to a maximum tax rate of 28%). Since Ana is not a dealer or "in the business" of selling collectibles, then the gain is typically treated as a capital gain and reported on Schedule D. Her gain is long-term because she purchased the toy two years ago, so she has held it longer than a year. Ana's gain is figured as follows:

| Gross sales price | $9,700 |
|---|---|
| Sales commission to the auction website | ($970) |
| Cost basis (original purchase price) | ($25) |
| **Gain on the sale** | **$8,705** |

**85. The answer is B.** Only the interest Judd receives from tax-exempt municipal bonds will need to be reported on his tax return, even though the interest is not taxable. He does not have to report any of the interest income on his traditional IRA on his tax return. Interest on insurance dividends left on deposit with the U.S. Department of Veterans Affairs is nontaxable interest and not reportable. The interest on HSA funds grows on a tax-free basis. Interest earned on an HSA is not considered taxable income when the funds are used for eligible medical expenses.

**86. The answer is A.** The amount of Monica's qualifying medical expenses is $6,200. Monica can deduct only the amount of their medical expenses that exceed 7.5% of her AGI ($93,600 × 7.5% = $7,020.) Since the total amount of her medical expenses are **lower** than 7.5% of her AGI, she is not allowed any medical expense deduction.

**87. The answer is A.** The Additional Medicare Tax of 0.9% applies to wages, compensation, tips, and self-employment income above specified threshold amounts. Distributions from qualified retirement plans, pension income, and other types of retirement income are exempt from this tax. Employer contributions to a qualified plan are also exempt.

**88. The answer is C.** Shannon must wait a minimum of ten years before claiming the EITC again. If the IRS examines a taxpayer's return and disallows all or part of the EITC, the taxpayer:

- Must pay back the amount in error with interest;
- May need to file Form 8862, *Information to Claim Earned Income Credit after Disallowance*;
- Cannot claim the EITC for the next two years if the IRS determines the error is because of reckless or intentional disregard of the rules; or
- Cannot claim the EITC for the next ten years if the IRS determines the error is because of fraud.

**89. The answer is B**, figured as follows:

| | |
|---|---|
| Rodney's wages | $32,000 |
| Interest on annuity | $100 |
| Rodney's gross income on his MFJ return | $32,100 |

Rodney must report his wages as well as the interest income. Life insurance proceeds are generally not taxable to a beneficiary, so the life insurance is not taxable or reportable, but any interest earned on the policy would be taxable. Incidentally, Crystal also has a filing requirement, but because Rodney remarried before the end of the tax year, Crystal's final tax return would be MFS. Her executor would be responsible for filing and signing Crystal's final tax return.

**90. The answer is B.** Rodolfo can deduct the cost of the alcohol treatment center, including meals and lodging, as a qualified medical expense. A taxpayer can include in medical expenses amounts paid for an inpatient's treatment at a therapeutic center for alcohol addiction. This includes meals and lodging provided by the center during treatment. A taxpayer can also include in medical expenses amounts paid for transportation to and from Alcoholics Anonymous meetings, if the attendance is pursuant to medical advice that membership in Alcoholics Anonymous is necessary for the treatment of a disease involving the excessive use of alcohol.

**91. The answer is C.** The donor is generally responsible for filing the gift tax return and paying any gift tax. Since Angelica died before she could file her returns, her executor must file the return.

**92. The answer is D.** Gerry would be required to include the tax-exempt interest in the calculation of his household income. For the purposes of the Premium Tax Credit, "household income" is the taxpayer's adjusted gross income on the federal income tax return plus: any excluded foreign income, nontaxable Social Security benefits, and tax-exempt interest. It does not include *Supplemental* Security Income (SSI), child support, disaster relief assistance payments, inheritances, or other types of exempt or excluded income. The calculation of household income also includes that of a spouse (if filing as MFJ) as well as for any dependents claimed on the return that are required to file their own tax return (but would not include a dependent that files an income tax return only for the purposes of claiming a refund of withheld income tax or estimated tax). Household income does not include the income of a person who is not claimed as a dependent, even if they live in the same household as the taxpayer. Also, Supplemental Security Income (SSI) is separate and different from regular social security income. SSI is generally only available to those at least 65 years old, or blind, or disabled with very limited assets and relatively low income.

**93. The answer is B.** Janessa's tentative QBI deduction is (20% × $80,000 = $16,000). The Section 199A "Qualified Business Income" deduction provides taxpayers a deduction for qualified business income from a qualified trade or business operated directly or through a pass-through entity. Eligible taxpayers may be entitled to a deduction of up to 20% of qualified business income (QBI) from a domestic business operated as a sole proprietorship or through a partnership, S corporation, trust, or estate. While the QBI deduction is subject to a limitation of 20% of modified taxable income (pre-QBI deduction taxable income, less any long-term capital gains and qualified dividends), here Janessa's modified taxable income was $107,000, and 20% of $107,000 = $21,400, which is more than $16,000.

**94. The answer is C.** Stacey may deduct the mortgage interest she incurred on both homes. ($14,500 + $3,000 = **$17,500**). She cannot deduct the loan interest on the land. A taxpayer can take the mortgage interest deduction on up to two homes.[40]

**95. The answer is B.** Rupert's qualified educational expenses are $4,400 ($4,000 tuition + $400 required textbooks). The definition of "qualified tuition and expenses" includes expenditures for course materials. The term "course materials" means books, supplies, and equipment needed for a course, whether or not the materials are purchased directly from the educational institution. The cost of health insurance is not a qualified higher education expense, including student health fees. The cost of housing is also not a qualified educational expense for the purposes of the American Opportunity Tax Credit (question modified from an IRS VITA tax training question).

---

[40] A taxpayer cannot deduct interest on land that they are holding, even with the intent to build a home on it. However, some interest may be deductible once construction begins. See Publication 936, Home Mortgage Interest Deduction, for more information on this topic.

**96. The answer is D.** For 2023, the federal adoption tax credit is $15,950. Henrietta is allowed to take the full adoption credit of $15,950, even though she only has $4,000 in qualifying expenses because the child is special needs. *However*, the adoption credit is a nonrefundable credit; any credit in excess of tax liability may be carried forward for up to five years. The amount of the credit she would be allowed to claim is therefore limited to her actual tax liability **($5,000)**. She may carryover any unused credits to future tax years.

> **Note:** The full amount of the adoption credit is allowed for a special-needs child as long as the adoption is a domestic adoption of a U.S. special-needs child (i.e., it cannot be a foreign adoption, although foreign adoptions are still eligible for the regular Adoption Credit, based on actual adoption expenses).

**97. The answer is D.** Kathleen can make tax-free charitable gifts of up to a total of $100,000 per year from her traditional IRA as a qualified charitable distribution (QCD). Although she will not be able to *deduct* her charitable contributions from the IRA in 2023, she is still allowed to withdraw a maximum contribution of $100,000 for any qualified charity she wishes.[41]

**98. The answer is C.** Kiyoshi must pay at least 110% of the tax liability on his prior year's tax return in order to meet the safe harbor rule for estimated tax payments. A higher-income taxpayer with an adjusted gross income of $150,000 or more ($75,000 or more if married filing separately) will not be assessed an estimated tax penalty if he pays the smaller of 90% of the tax liability on his current year return or *110%* of the tax liability on his prior-year tax return. This contrasts with a taxpayer earning *less than* $150,000, who can rely on a *lower* safe harbor rule by paying the *lesser* of: 90% of the tax liability on his current year return or 100% of the tax liability on his prior-year return. A taxpayer also will not face an underpayment penalty if the total tax shown on his return (minus the amounts of tax credits or paid through withholding) is less than $1,000.

**99. The answer is D.** Funeral expenses are never deductible on an individual tax return. All the other expenses listed are allowable as an itemized deduction on Schedule A.

**100. The answer is A.** In order for a noncustodial parent to claim a child, the custodial parent must sign Form 8332, *Release and Revocation of Release of Claim to Exemption for Child by Custodial Parent* (or a substantially similar statement), that they will not claim the child as a dependent for the year. The noncustodial parent then attaches the form to his or her individual return. For more information, see Publication 501, *Exemptions, Standard Deduction, and Filing Information*.

---

[41] A QCD is a direct transfer of funds from an IRA to a qualified charity. It must be a direct transfer. In other words, the taxpayer must direct their IRA trustee to make a distribution directly from their IRA to the charity. The IRA trustee will report the distribution on IRS Form 1099-R. For a QCD to count as a taxpayer's current year RMD, the funds must be distributed to the charity by the IRA trustee by the RMD deadline, which is generally December 31.

*This page intentionally left blank.*

# About the Authors

### Joel Busch, CPA, JD

Joel Busch is a tax professor at San Jose State University, where he teaches courses at both the graduate and undergraduate levels. Previously, he was in charge of tax audits, research, and planning for one of the largest civil construction and mining companies in the United States. He received both a BS in Accounting and a MS in Taxation from SJSU and he has a JD from the Monterey College of Law. He is licensed in California as both a CPA and an attorney.

### Christy Pinheiro, EA, ABA®

Christy Pinheiro is an Enrolled Agent, Accredited Business Advisor®, and bestselling financial writer. She is a graduate of San Jose State University. Christy worked as an accountant for the state of California as well as two private CPA firms before going into private practice. She is the author of multiple books on taxation, bookkeeping, and tax practice management. Her finance and tax articles have been nationally published.

### Thomas A. Gorczynski, EA, USTCP

Thomas A. Gorczynski is an Enrolled Agent, a Certified Tax Planner, and admitted to the bar of the United States Tax Court. Tom is also a nationally known tax educator and currently serves as editor-in-chief of EA Journal. He received the 2019 Excellence in Education Award from the National Association of Enrolled Agents. He earned a Master of Science in Taxation from Golden Gate University and a Certificate in Finance and Accounting from the Wharton School at the University of Pennsylvania.

See more information on our official website: *www.PassKeyOnline.com.*

*This page intentionally left blank.*

Made in the USA
Coppell, TX
20 April 2024

31507193R00098